WAR-TORN ECOLOGIES, AN-ARCHIC FRAGMENTS

Cultural Inquiry

EDITED BY CHRISTOPH F. E. HOLZHEY
AND MANUELE GRAGNOLATI

The series 'Cultural Inquiry' is dedicated to exploring how diverse cultures can be brought into fruitful rather than pernicious confrontation. Taking culture in a deliberately broad sense that also includes different discourses and disciplines, it aims to open up spaces of inquiry, experimentation, and intervention. Its emphasis lies in critical reflection and in identifying and highlighting contemporary issues and concerns, even in publications with a historical orientation. Following a decidedly cross-disciplinary approach, it seeks to enact and provoke transfers among the humanities, the natural and social sciences, and the arts. The series includes a plurality of methodologies and approaches, binding them through the tension of mutual confrontation and negotiation rather than through homogenization or exclusion.

Christoph F. E. Holzhey is the Founding Director of the ICI Berlin Institute for Cultural Inquiry. Manuele Gragnolati is Professor of Italian Literature at the Sorbonne Université in Paris and Associate Director of the ICI Berlin.

WAR-TORN ECOLOGIES,
AN-ARCHIC FRAGMENTS
Reflections from the Middle East

EDITED BY
UMUT YILDIRIM

ISBN (Hardcover): 978-3-96558-052-7
ISBN (Paperback): 978-3-96558-053-4
ISBN (PDF): 978-3-96558-054-1
ISBN (EPUB): 978-3-96558-055-8

Cultural Inquiry, 27
ISSN (Print): 2627-728X
ISSN (Online): 2627-731X

Bibliographical Information of the German National Library
The German National Library lists this publication in the Deutsche
Nationalbibliografie (German National Bibliography); detailed
bibliographic information is available online at http://dnb.d-nb.de.

In Europe, volumes are printed by Lightning Source UK Ltd., Milton
Keynes, UK. See the final page for further details.

Digital editions can be viewed and downloaded freely at:
https://doi.org/10.37050/ci-27.

ICI Berlin Press is an imprint of
ICI gemeinnütziges Institut für Cultural Inquiry Berlin GmbH
Christinenstr. 18/19, Haus 8
D-10119 Berlin
publishing@ici-berlin.org
www.ici-berlin.org

Contents

Foreword by Françoise Vergès

The essays in *War-torn Ecologies, An-archic Fragments: Reflections from the Middle East*, edited by Umut Yıldırım, could not have arrived at a better moment. Indeed, the consequences of the state of permanent war that capitalism, racism, colonialism, and all forms of imperialism are waging upon peoples and the planet are now closely studied by scholars, artists, scientists, and activists. The contributors to this volume — scholars and artists — propose an 'imaginative methodological exercise in thinking through the multispecies actualities and afterlives of war-torn worlds in the Middle East'.[1] Looking at specific cases but avoiding exceptionalism, they examine the possibilities of 'war-torn ecologies', which Umut Yıldırım describes as 'an ecologically infused aesthetical stance and political perspective that seeks to unsettle the geographical profiling of the Middle East'.[2] The Middle East is thus not simply a site of sectarian violence, of petroleum capitalism and a dumping ground of imperialist debris, but a site where ecological practices are imagined.

The contributions are exceptional because they remain close to the ground and open to the ways in which people interpret how wars are impacting their lives and environment, but they do not do this through an ethnological gaze. They reject the 'romantic gesture

---

1   Umut Yıldırım, 'War-torn Ecologies: Human and More-than-Human Intersections of Ethnography and the Arts', in this volume, pp. 1–25 (p. 2).
2   Ibid., p. 5.

toward vibrancy and authenticity'.[3] War-torn ecologies are abolitionist geographies; they practice what Ruth Wilson Gilmore has called 'life in rehearsal, not a recitation of rules, much less a relentless lament'[4] but a 'historical geography of the future', building what feminist activist and author Leanne Betasamosake Simpson calls 'constellations of coresistance' that 'affirm[...] life and world-making in a time of acute racial violence'.[5] Rehearsing life because 'we are constituted through and by continued vulnerability to overwhelming force though not *only* known to ourselves and to each other *by* that force', as Christina Sharpe has written.[6]

The authors introduce us to haunted wells, djins, ghouls, goats and goatherds, herbs and politics of the commons, toxicity by non-living agents, and tales that make sense of the world that wars make. The authors explore what Rob Nixon has analysed in *Slow Violence and the Environmentalism of the Poor*,[7] in which he discussed the inattention to the 'attritional lethality of many environmental crises, in contrast with the sensational, spectacle-driven messaging that impels public activism

---

3   Ibid.
4   Excerpt from Ruth Wilson Gilmore, *Abolition on Stolen Land*, online video recording of the keynote address of the public programme 'Sanctuary Spaces: Reworlding Humanism', 9 October 2020, UCLA Luskin Institute on Inequality and Democracy, Vimeo <https://vimeo.com/467484872#t=28:14s> [accessed 24 March 2022].
5   Robyn Maynard and Leanne Betasamosake Simpson, *Rehearsals for Living* (Chicago, IL: Haymarket, 2022), p. 7. See also Leanne Betasamosake Simpson, *As We Have Always Done: Indigenous Freedom Through Radical Resistance* (Minneapolis: University of Minnesota Press, 2017), chapter 12, 'Constellations of Coresistance', pp. 211–31.
6   Christina Sharpe, *In the Wake: On Blackness and Being* (Durham, NC: Duke University Press, 2016), p. 16.
7   Rob Nixon, *Slow Violence and the Environmentalism of the Poor* (Cambridge, MA: Harvard University Press, 2013).

today'.[8] But what I think makes the book necessary reading is its feminist approach to the world that war has made, and continues to make, in the Middle East, a region whose realities are masked behind so many clichés — veiled women, terrorism, traditions, lack of democracy.

THE POLITICS OF UN-BREATHING: DREAD, STRESS, LUNGS

Even when we do not want to yield to a catastrophic ideology that produces powerlessness, we cannot ignore a sense of dread caused by the Covid-19 pandemic and the daily assaults of racism, capitalism, genocide, colonial occupation, dispossession, wars, femicide, imperialism, xenophobic nationalism, fascism, Islamophobia, performative anti-racism, liberal multiculturalism, climate disaster, and civilizing feminism. As the 2022 Intergovernmental Panel on Climate Change (IPCC) report announced 'widespread, pervasive impacts to ecosystems, people, settlements, and infrastructure'[9] in the near future and especially in the Global South and we observed governments choosing to remain deaf to the warnings, the weapons industry continuing to flourish, and extraction and exploitation ceaselessly ravaging the planet, it was understandable that some of us had a hard time processing such an appetite for destruction and death. When I experience this feeling, I tell myself that I need to look the monster in the face, at all its features in

---

8   Ibid.
9   Hans-Otto Pörtner, Debra C. Roberts, and others, 'IPCC, 2022: Summary for Policymakers', in *Climate Change 2022: Impacts, Adaptation, and Vulnerability; Contribution of Working Group II to the Sixth Assessment Report of the Intergovernmental Panel on Climate Change*, ed. by Hans-Otto Pörtner, Debra C. Roberts, and others (Cambridge: Cambridge University Press, forthcoming) <https://www.ipcc.ch/report/ar6/wg2/downloads/report/IPCC_AR6_WGII_SummaryForPolicymakers.pdf> [accessed 22 March 2022].

all their heinous configurations, and not be petrified; to transform dread into anger, into the desire to fight back, into a place to conspire: Where is the monster vulnerable? Where to throw a stone to stop the machine? How to organize? The authors have no fear, they have looked the monster in the face. They show how capitalism, racism, and imperialism are making the world uninhabitable. 'I Can't Breathe', which has become the rallying cry against police violence worldwide, also brings to light the politics of un-breathing and the suffocating effects of capitalism and im-perialism, the systemic and structural violence that denies the right to breathe to peoples of colour. According to the World Health Organization (WHO), 'Air pollution is one of the greatest environmental risk to health.'[10] Air pollu-tion causes millions of premature deaths every year, largely as a result of increased mortality from stroke, heart disease, chronic obstructive pulmonary disease, lung cancer, and acute respiratory infections.[11] More and more babies in the Global South are born with respiratory disease, making them vulnerable to premature death as children and adults. More and more children are dying of asthma, a condition that is easy to cure.

'War makes atmosphere', Kali Rabaii writes. She de-scribes how non-living, more-than-human agents left be-hind by armies harm human and more-than-human lives, polluting and contaminating land, water, air, and bodies. War ecologies deeply affect women's wombs, and babies are born with birth defects. War makes the womb into a threat. Can we then talk of *pre-natal death*, by which I

---

10   'Ambient (Outdoor) Air Pollution', website of the World Health Organization (WHO), 19 December 2022 <https://www.who.int/news-room/fact-sheets/detail/ambient-(outdoor)-air-quality-and-health> [accessed 21 June 2023].

11   Ibid.

mean the fact that before a child is even born, she/he is already condemned to premature death? Its healthy development is threatened in the womb of the black, indigenous, Arab, or brown woman whose life is threatened by poverty, lack of proper food, clean water, and air, and lack of pre- and post-natal care. In the Global South and among poor minorities in the North, babies are born with many more diseases than those born in white and bourgeois families, especially respiratory diseases (they can't properly breathe). In other words, the more children of the rich are protected, by laws and forms of care, the more children of the Global South are denied childhood. This is not a paradox. It is the result of a political choice: some children are deemed worthy of the right to a good childhood while others not only are denied childhood but are treated as adults, abandoned and criminalized. Palestinian legal scholar Nadera Shalhoub-Kervorkian has described as the politics of *un-childing,* the 'understanding of children as political capital in the hands of those in power, the political work of violence designed to create, direct, govern, transform, and construct colonized children as dangerous, racialized others, enabling their eviction from the realm of childhood itself'.[12]

Racial and class politics of un-breathing mean that the lungs of humans and of the planet are under attack. They are suffocating. Trees, fish, rivers, seas, lakes, and ani-

---

12   See Nadera Shalhoub-Kervorkian, *Incarcerated Childhood and the Politics of Unchilding* (Cambridge: Cambridge University Press, 2019); Heidi Morrison, 'Review of Nadera Shalhoub-Kervorkian, Incarcerated Childhood and the Politics of Unchilding', *Journal of Palestine Studies,* 49.3 (Spring 2020), pp. 82–84 <https://www.palestine-studies.org/en/node/1650365> [accessed 22 March 2022]; Sarah Sheriff, 'Unchilding of Palestinian Children', *Muslim News,* 28 June 2018 <https://muslimnews.co.uk/newspaper/human-rights/unchilding-palestinian-children/> [accessed 22 March 2022].

mals cannot breathe. There is a worldwide crisis of breathing. The definition of racism by Ruth Wilson Gilmore, as the fabrication of 'group differentiated vulnerabilities to premature death in distinct yet densely connected political geographies' has never resonated so truly.[13] She remarks that racism as a form of structural selectivity among humans correlates with the 'technology of antirelationality' that racial capitalism creates, by which she means that 'collective life in humanity is separated and then reconnected in ways that feed the production of capital and wealth'.[14]

THE POLITICS OF TOXICITY AND POISONING

The colonial/racial fabrication of landscapes along the lines of clean/unclean, preserved/abandoned is explored by Nadine Hattom in 'Great Sand: Grains of Occupation and Representation'. Telling us that military training areas cover 6 percent of the earth's land mass (which means we have to add all the maritime zones to get a better view of the occupation of the planet as a military training space), Hattom shows how military landscapes are constructed with intent.[15] She questions the military's claim that its training grounds are good environmental politics since plants and animals are not disturbed by human activity. She raises an important question: In resisting militarization, what to show and what not to show? Hattom does not wish to give centre stage to the occupying US army in Iraq. She removes

---

13   Ruth Wilson Gilmore, *Golden Gulag: Prisons, Surplus, Crisis, and Opposition in Globalizing California* (Berkeley: University of California Press, 2006), p. 28.

14   See Jodi Melamed, 'Diagnosing Racial Capitalism', *Boston Review*, 10 September 2018 <https://bostonreview.net/forum_response/andrew-douglas-diagnosing-racial-capitalism/> [accessed 22 March 2022].

15   Nadine Hattom, 'Great Sand: Grains of Occupation and Representation', in this volume, p. 119.

the soldiers from a series of archival photographs of Operation Iraqi Freedom and from photographs of training sites in Germany to challenge the naturalization of a military presence. Whether they walk along dunes or through an oasis, their walk is not just an ordinary walk. They learn to walk in order to kill. They do not inhabit these spaces innocently. Hattom also looks at the argument that training grounds protect natural habitat since they are remote from civilian activities that are said to be more invasive and disruptive than military practice.[16] When military landscapes, which, as Hattom observes, are 'constructed with intent',[17] are made into sites of nature conservation and preservation, the imperialist, occupying army becomes the protector of nature. What precedes its occupation of landscape is hidden — the weapons industry, the training of men and women into machines to rape, maim, and kill, the high degree of contamination and pollution caused by the fabrication of weapons and their use. The civilians become a threat; nature is shown as being able to repair itself, so why stop the creation of waste? According to the World Bank, eleven million tons of solid waste are produced every day

---

16   There is a literature on Cold War landscapes, nature preservation, and even tourism; see James Card, 'Paradise in No Man's Land', *Earth Island Journal*, 23.1 (Spring 2008): *The Argicultural Issue*, pp. 51–54 <https://www.earthisland.org/journal/index.php/magazine/entry/paradise_in_no_mans_land/> [accessed 22 March 2022]; Peter Coates, 'Borderland, No-Man's Land, Nature's Wonderland', *Environment and History*, 20.4 (November 2014), pp. 499–516. On Cold War landscapes, see *The Cold War in the Heart Land*, a web resource created by faculty and graduate students and hosted by the Center for Russian, East European, and Eurasian Studies at the University of Kansas <https://coldwarheartland.ku.edu/landscapes> [accessed 22 March 2022]. Cold War landscapes have been made into sites of tourism; see Keun-Sik Jung, 'The Construction of the Cold War Landscape and Tourism: The Possibilities and Limitations of its Peaceful Use', *Journal of Asian Sociology*, 48.3 (September 2019), pp. 287–319

17   Hattom, 'Great Sand', p. 114.

in the world. Although they only account for 16% of the world's population, high-income countries collectively generate more than a third of the world's waste. It is not clear if this data takes into account the huge amount of waste generated by imperialist armies, but capitalism is clearly the prime producer of waste. Waste 'is a sign of capitalism's success', Fred Magdoff and Chris Williams have argued.[18] All that 'the enormous economic financial sector does is find ways to make money with money, providing little of social value', they add. The military industry is an economy of waste, waste of the huge amount of energy it needs to be fabricated and run; it leaves behind wasted lands and wasted bodies, it has no social value whatsoever. It feeds a masculinity that is educated to rape, kill, and maim. The success of capitalism as waste's producer is measured by the capacity to make the white world clean and externalize its waste.

As states deliberately dump garbage in poor neighbourhoods and build dumping grounds near them, imperialist armies deliberately dipose of their toxic waste in countries they invade or occupy. The relation between colonization, racism, and creating dirty, polluted, contaminated spaces is historical, linked with slavery and colonization. But we have examples today, too. For instance, during its siege of Gaza in 2007, the State of Israel dumped untreated sewage into the sea, producing a visual culture of contrasting images: on the Israeli side, a dreamy vision of Mediterranean beaches; on the Palestinian side, overcrowded beaches as sewage dump. White Mediterranean vs. Black–Arab Mediterranean. The racialized visual

18   Fred Magdoff and Chris Williams, 'Capitalist Economies Create Waste, Not Social Value', *Truthout*, 17 August 2017 <https://truthout.org/articles/capitalist-economies-create-waste-not-social-value/> [accessed 22 March 2022].

culture of clean vs. dirty, of protected nature vs. nature destroyed by the uneducated poor, perpetuates the idea of a civilized/clean white world vs. an uncivilized/dirty black and brown planet.

THE IRREPARABLE AND THE POLITICS OF REPAIR

Will it be possible to repair the accumulated layers of devastation inflicted by genocides, massacres, slavery, colonization, and plantations, agro-business, monoculture, extraction, dispossession, exploitation, wars, and racism? The 'open veins' (to borrow Eduardo Galeano's expression)[19] of the planet, the dreadful scars — memories and histories erased, personal and collective suffering, exile, deportation, exploitation, dispossession, the destroyed archives, abandoned mines leaving huge mountains of dust and huge holes, the coasts forever damaged by resorts, cities, privatization, the deep seas forever disturbed by extraction, the discarded industrial factories, the bombed cities; we will have to live with some irreparability. But, as writer and poet Keguro Macharia has observed, the irreparable does not need to be eschatological.[20] The irreparable is not an end. Ruins are not ruination, though this is not to celebrate the aesthetics of ruin. What this collection of essays shows is that we cannot ignore the multiplication of zones of non-being whose creation Frantz Fanon connected with colonialism and racism. A line is traced, Fanon argued, above which there is the zone of being, where the full humanity of 'humans' is socially recognized through human, civil, and labour rights; below that line is the *zone of non-being*,

---

19   Eduardo Galeano, *The Open Veins of Latin America: Five Centuries of the Pillage of a Continent*, trans. by Cedric Belfrage (New York: Monthly Review Press, 1973).

20   In an online conversation I shared with him and Christina Sharpe on 17 February 2022.

where those who are considered sub-human or more-than-human live, their humanity either not recognized or put into question. Caribbean philosopher Sylvia Wynter has called the figure that embodies that line *Man*, an exclusionary European representation that precludes other ways of being human.[21] What Munira Khayyat describes in 'Of Goats and Bombs: How to Live (and Die) in an Explosive Landscape' is a zone of non-being created by the Israeli army. Khayyat tells the story of a goatherd, Abu Bilal, who, despite the danger presented by the thousands of cluster bombs the Israeli army has dumped on the region, wants to continue to follow his goats through fields and hills, goats being known to be able to survive periods of scarcity and, most crucially, being light-footed enough not to trigger the cluster bombs that Israel rained on the roads, valleys, villages, towns, orchards, fields, gardens, and homes of Southern Lebanon. We learn in passing that the 4.6 million cluster bombs the Israeli army dropped were expired stock inherited from the US war against the Vietnamese. Military technologies of death are recycled, since laying waste upon land and body is a market and money must be made. Hence, we could map the deadly market of cluster bombs that have contaminated Vietnam, Laos, Sri Lanka, Cambodia, Congo, South Lebanon, Afghanistan, Iraq, and Syria, from the factory where they are fabricated to the barracks where they are stored, to the planes that carry them, and along with these places all those who are involved in the market of death: businessmen, engineers, middlemen, soldiers, truck drivers, handlers, pilots. An entire economy whose workings and structure are much more hidden than

---

21   Sylvia Wynter, 'Unsettling the Coloniality of Being/Power/Truth/ Freedom: Towards the Human After Man, Its Overrepresentation — An Argument', *CR: The New Centennial Review*, 3.3 (Fall 2003), pp. 257–337 <https://doi.org/10.1353/ncr.2004.0015>.

those of other deadly economies, like oil or minerals. Why
is that so? It is a huge market that amounts to billions of
US dollars[22] with huge investments,[23] with leading produ-
cers and sellers, among them the US, France, and Russia.
The cluster bomb that killed the goatherd Ali in 2005 had
a history. And yet, as Khayyat shows, life has a place in
the landscape of war where goatherds are caught between
Israeli and Palestinian soldiers. There is a slow resistance to
the speedy death brought by cluster bombs. Lives are lost,
but the everyday fight for life is 'life in rehearsal'.[24]

WAR-TORN ECOLOGIES

Throughout the essays, we learn about de-poisoning practices and the kind of fragments of repair that artist Kader
Attia has said are 'about shaping a possibility of emer-

---

22 See the site of Stockholm International Peace Research Institute
     for data <https://www.sipri.org/media/press-release/2018/global-
     arms-industry-us-companies-dominate-top-100-russian-arms-
     industry-moves-second-place> [accessed 22 March 2022].

23 Consider Gillian Rich, 'The Best Defense Stocks for Today — and
     the Future', *Investor's Business Daily*, 14 March 2022 <https://www.
     investors.com/news/best-defense-stocks-to-buy/>   [accessed   22
     March 2022]; Lou Whiteman, 'Investing in Defense Stocks', *The
     Motley Fool*, 22 March 2022 <https://www.fool.com/investing/stock-
     market/market-sectors/industrials/defense-stocks/>   [accessed   22
     March 2022]. Indeed, *US News and World Report* announced on its
     front page on 8 March 2022: 'Bank of America analyst Ronald Epstein.
     Epstein estimates that U.S. defense spending as a percentage of gross
     domestic product could rise from around 2.8% to between 3.5% and
     4% in response to the recent Russian aggression, and says there is
     likely upside to both U.S. and European defense budgets. Epstein
     is projecting at least $800 billion in U.S. defense spending in 2023,
     creating big opportunities for defense companies. Here are eight of the
     best defense stocks to buy now, according to Bank of America.' Wayne
     Duggan, 'Best Defense Stock to Buy Now', *US News and World Report*,
     8 March 2022 <https://money.usnews.com/investing/slideshows/
     best-defense-stocks-to-buy-now> [accessed 22 March 2022].

24 Gilmore, *Abolition on Stolen Land*.

ging into another reality, into another, more just world'.[25] Jumana Emil Abboud, Kali Rubaii, and Marwa Arsanios remind us that a poison is also its cure. '[T]he very spring waters that poisoned you will also set you free', Abboud writes.[26] The wonderful tales Abboud and Rubaii tell us are forms of what Umut Yıldırım calls in her essay 'eco-redaction', 'an aesthetic manoeuvre for thinking with erasure so as to uncover ecological clusters of destruction and transformation'.[27] The authors celebrate constellations of resistance in the war-torn worlds in the Middle East, that region which hegemonic powers have tried for centuries to shape and reshape. They fight against erasure and through an exposé of what the racist, colonial, imperialist monster is capable of, demonstrate that the patient daily work to maintain life constructs a world full of sensual acts, of tenderness and love. Building a politics of the commons, women and men in the Middle East, with their understanding of the social, political, and economic dimensions of struggle, trace, across time and space, spaces that strengthen our efforts everywhere in the world. They do not want to summon outrage and political consciousness through appeals that result in pity. When I read their essays, I saw the killings fields of Vietnam, Cambodia, Laos, the afterlives of US bombings to this day. I saw the mining of lithium, cobalt, copper; I saw the floods, the fires, the anti-

---

25 Kader Attia at the study programme *Fragments of Repair/La Colonie Nomade*, which I convened in Paris, April–July 2021. For the curriculum of this programme, see <https://www.bakonline.org/program-item/fragments-of-repair/fragments-of-repair-la-colonie-nomade/> [accessed 22 March 2022].

26 Jumana Emil Abboud, 'Hide Your Water from the Sun: A Performance for Spirited Waters', in this volume, pp. 121–38 (p. 132).

27 Umut Yıldırım, 'Mulberry Affects: Ecology, Memory, and Aesthetics on the Shores of the Tigris River in the Wake of Genocide', in this volume, pp. 27–66 (p. 29).

life politics against refugees in Europe and the US. I saw billionaires getting richer while the majority of humanity is getting poorer. But I also saw wonders, the fact that in the darkest hours of oppression and war, solidarity is active, roads are created, sanctuaries are opened.

Yet, as I write, I am reminded that not all war-torn worlds are equal in the eyes of hegemonic powers. I have recently heard journalists and politicians naturalizing racial difference between refugees when they talked about the millions of Ukrainian refugees fleeing their invaded country: 'This is not a place like Iraq or Afghanistan. This is a *relatively* [sic] civilized, relatively European country.' 'We're not talking about Syrians fleeing bombings, we are talking about Europeans leaving in their cars that look like us.'[28] This is how consent is fabricated to the racial division between 'good refugees' and 'bad refugees', between 'good' and 'bad' migrants.

In the uninhabitable world of racism, imperialism, patriarchy, and capitalism, the need for establishing spaces of freedom, spaces where transmission and imagination are fostered and encouraged, spaces to rest and recuperate, to prepare strategies and express love, have always been the first task of the wretched of the earth. *War-torn Ecologies, An-archic Fragments* contributes to that work. Read it and organize!

---

28   See e.g. Sarah Ellison and Travis M. Andrews, '"They Seem So Like Us": In Depicting Ukraine's plight, some in media use offensive comparisons', *The Washington Post*, 27 February 2022 <https://www. washingtonpost.com/media/2022/02/27/media-ukraine-offensive-comparisons/>.

War-torn Ecologies
Human and More-than-Human Intersections
of Ethnography and the Arts
UMUT YILDIRIM

Extinction looms on all sides, scientists agree, and it's becoming increasingly difficult to breathe. The current unfolding of the so-called Anthropocene has brought with it
widespread habitat loss and the poisoning of land, water,
air, and food, all of which is now amplified by the general
effects of climate change. Entire assemblages of life con-
taining humans, trees, animals, plants, rocks, and bodies
of water are breaking apart, threatening mutually bonded,
multispecies breathing relationships. But isn't the very concept of the Anthropocene an epistemological manoeuvre
that assumes 'a blanket humanity, a blanket history, and
a blanket geological record'?[1] Isn't this a racial term[2] that

---

1   Aaron Vansintjan, 'Going beyond the "Ecological Turn" in the Human-
     ities', *Entitle Blog — A Collaborative Writing Project on Political Ecol-
     ogy*, 2016 <https://entitleblog.org/2016/03/01/going-beyond-the-
     ecological-turn-in-the-humanities/> [accessed 26 July 2019].
2   Françoise Vergès, 'Racial Capitalocene: Is the Anthropocene Racial?',
     in *Futures of Black Radicalism*, ed. by Gaye Theresa Johnson and Alex
     Lubin (London: Verso Books, 2017), pp. 72–82.

eclipses the central role of colonial, genocidal, and militarist violence in its own formation? Multispecies constellations were being choked to death by mass violence in regimented geographies such as the Middle East long before talk of the Anthropocene achieved wide currency. Wars attack the lungs with full force in the Middle East, resistant breath emerging in the crevices of occupation through the wake of genocidal extinction across species.

War-torn Ecologies, An-archic Fragments: Reflections from the Middle East presents an imaginative methodological exercise in thinking through the multispecies actualities and afterlives of war-torn worlds in the Middle East with an attention to ecological processes that are deeply scarred by war. It embraces a methodology of 'montage'[3] that explores the intersection of ethnography and the arts, delivering an-archic fragments of the racialized, militarized, poisoned, neglected, yet resistant rhythms of Middle Eastern ecologies. Montage works here to juxtapose seemingly disparate histories, memories, feelings, and praxis that emerge from the 'Middle East', a term that refers here neither to a fixed geographical entity with clearly defined boundaries nor to some generic facsimile of an 'Arab world', but to a generative epistemological field that enables us to think together with ecological and affective fragments of organized mass violence, as well as endurance and resistance through the cracks of occupation under war. Montage has the capacity to counter the archival, legal, and commonsensical frameworks of sovereign states by paying attention to seemingly 'small events' that foreground relationships between the human and the more-than-human;

---

3   Françoise Vergès, 'Wandering Souls and Returning Ghosts: Writing the History of the Dispossessed', *Yale French Studies*, 118/119 (2010), pp. 136–54 (p. 136).

between the geographical and the racialized; between captivity, endurance, and praxis; between the affective, the ecological, and the aesthetical; and between anthropology and the arts.

The an-archic fragments offered within this volume are methodologically vitalized by thinking with 'refusal'.[4] Its spirit is energized by Audra Simpson's work on settler colonialism and indigenous sovereignty in North America, where she meditates on how settler colonialism has temporally severed the pre-contact connectedness that indigenous nationals had with land and among themselves, eroding their capacity to build coalitions. In the case of the Iroquois, where settler citizenship grants 'gifts' of belonging to citizens in the form of passports and simultaneously denies them sovereignty over land, indigenous nationals negotiate their co-existence with settler membership or refuse and undermine the project altogether. This refusal of power asymmetries is given life by rituals that co-cultivate 'care for and defence of territory'.[5] Similarly, contributions in this volume meditate on political and aesthetical choreographies that disrupt structures and apparatuses of colonial and genocidal *arche*. They refuse to be silenced and erased by 'the logic of *arche*'[6] that combines 'to begin', 'to lead', and 'to rule', and 'that presupposes a determinate superiority exercised upon an equally determinate inferiority'.[7] The an-archic fragments that we convey here refuse to take for granted the violently eclipsed facts produced

---

4   Audra Simpson, *Mohawk Interruptus: Political Life Across the Borders of Settler States* (Durham, NC: Duke University Press, 2014).

5   Ibid., p. 3.

6   Jacques Rancière, 'Ten Theses on Politics', trans. by Davide Panagia and Rachel Bowlby, *Theory & Event*, 5.3 (2001) <https://doi.org/10.1353/tae.2001.0028>.

7   Ibid.

by colonial apparatuses and their archival and supremacist myths of origin. They seek to mobilize ethnographic and artistic creativity in order to push back against 'debilitating' processes of colonial and imperialist mass violence, and to become 'infinitely demanding'[8] of autonomy.

Debilitation under conditions of settler colonialism, argues Jasbir Puar, works as a 'capacitating frame' that legally (and geopolitically) recognizes some injuries at the expense of others by virtue of state recognition and allows the 'deployment of maiming' as a central tactic of settler colonialism in order to occupy.[9] That is, for those who are positioned as 'a source of value extraction' for the maintenance of settler orders, debilitation involves 'a slow wearing down of populations', which works as an affective threat resulting from the immediacy and expediency of state-sovereign violence.[10] In this logic, certain worlds possess an almost 'natural' capacity to be deficient and disposable, thus providing justification for ongoing occupation and ecocide of brown geographies. In this volume's contributions, an-archic montage refuses the terms of such 'capacitating frames'. Rather than functioning as a representational ecological descriptor of a unified Middle Eastern consciousness with a self-Orientalizing twist, or indeed an uninterrupted position of geographical wholeness and political solidarity, the notion of war-torn ecologies employed here takes as its point of departure the incommensurability of our experiences throughout wars and the ruptures that colonial occupation and genocide denialism mass produce, not only in territories where we live, work, and/or tend, but

---

8　　Simon Critchley, *Infinitely Demanding: Ethics of Commitment, Politics of Resistance* (London: Verso Books, 2007).

9　　Jasbir K. Puar, *The Right to Maim: Debility, Capacity, Disability* (Durham, NC: Duke University Press, 2017), p. xvi.

10　　Ibid., pp. xviii and xiv.

also in the diaspora where those of us privileged enough to have fled the settings and politics of war have recommenced life and rebuilt homes in new lands.

Our disparate and incommensurable paths enable us to co-create a political and aesthetical space in which to foreground the role of racialized 'moods'[11] — and, we add, geographically profiled, ecologically and spiritually inflicted, and temporally regimented war-torn feelings — that are both shaped by the multiaxial force of state-sponsored mass-scale violence and that shape everyday ecological resurgence. 'Racializing affect',[12] this volume represents an ecologically infused aesthetical stance and political perspective that seeks to unsettle the geographical profiling of the Middle East as a spectacular and exotic repertoire of sectarian and primordial violence, an empty signifier for petroleum capitalism, and the dumping ground of imperialist debris. The communality of our work is nestled in the act of turning creativity itself into a ritual of refusal by 'dwelling on the negative'[13] and thinking through feelings that 'break' from and push back against colonial occupation and its ecocide and against whitewashed epistemologies that insist on the act of rendering things static, settled, and resolvable. It is not just the brutal and acute transformation of life into corpses as a result of war that this volume positions itself against, but also the insidiously mundane, non-spectacular, and unexceptional 'debilitat-

---

11   Lisa M. Corrigan, *Black Feelings: Race and Affect in the Long Sixties* (Jackson: University Press of Mississippi, 2020), p. xiv.

12   Ulla D. Berg and Ana Y. Ramos-Zayas, 'Racializing Affect: A Theoretical Proposition', *Current Anthropology*, 56.5 (2015), pp. 654–77 <https://doi.org/10.1086/683053>; Puar, *The Right to Maim*.

13   Glen Sean Coulthard, *Red Skin, White Masks: Rejecting the Colonial Politics of Recognition* (Minneapolis: University of Minnesota Press, 2014), p. 110.

ing' effects of 'the geopolitics of race'.[14] Rather than forcing
aesthetical inquiry into an analytical straitjacket that takes
the stability of legal systems for granted and amplifies the
vitality of interspecies relationality by assigning to it exotic
horizons decipherable only by the inquiry's participants
and the anthropologist, this volume problematizes the very
assumptions of legal stability that colour contemporary
thinking about disastrous worlds under the so-called Anthropocene. To think through war-torn ecologies is to position creativity *against* accounts that refuse to acknowledge
that some worlds have always already been destroyed, that
occupation and war are endemic, and that despite all this,
endurance, resurgence, and eco-praxis continue. The contributions here gesture toward a 'brown commons'[15] as the
commons of 'brown people, places, feelings, sounds, animals, minerals, flora and other objects'; a commons made
of human and more-than-human lives and things, entangled through a history of destruction and in response to it;
a commons of brown breath whose flow has been slowed
and disrupted by mass violence, yet has never lost a resistant pulse.

AFFECTIVE ECOLOGY

Analytical attention to affective ecology has been adopted
in anthropology, the arts, and environmental humanities
as a way of thinking not about, but *together with*, the ecological elements of long-term destruction and resurgence
that have resulted a 'human-caused environmental catastrophe'. Following Donna Haraway's invitation to under-

---

14   Puar, *The Right to Maim*, p. 55.
15   José Esteban Muñoz, *The Sense of Brown*, ed. by Joshua Chambers-
      Letson and Tavia Nyong'o (Durham, NC: Duke University Press
      Books, 2020).

stand becoming as 'becoming with' species with whom humans co-inhabit the world and Tsing's call for 'noticing' unexpected life forms that emerge amidst capitalist wreckage within the larger context of climate change,[16] a new genre of affective thinking with ecology emerged. This genre of affective ecology positions itself against humancentric postulates where the human is endowed with extraordinary and exclusive cognitive capacities that transcend the natural world. They advocate instead for an ecologically infused percipience that is better equipped to confront both the analytical separation of human from other-thanhuman and the hierarchical postulate of life in which only humans have the capacity to feel, know, and think. This approach proposes that the political, rather than being distinct from the natural order, is always already intertwined with it, an analytical distinction that renders majoritarian politics' claims to separation from the natural order subject to analysis. The political, we learn, emerges in the interstices and crevices of rational politics, shedding light on a new political sensorium wherein humans are deeply enmeshed in and forge political alliances with more-thanhuman others, from inanimate rocks endowed with spiritual capacities to rivers that are accepted as the ancestral kin of indigenous folk. At the same time that these interstices and crevices expose the magnitude of extinction under the so-called Anthropocene, they also point up imaginative pathways toward thinking with those fragmented ecological forms that unexpectedly regenerate themselves despite the scale of mass destruction.

16 Donna J. Haraway, *When Species Meet* (Minneapolis: University of Minnesota Press, 2008), p. 244; Anna Lowenhaupt Tsing, *The Mushroom at the End of the World: On the Possibility of Life in Capitalist Ruins* (Princeton, NJ: Princeton University Press, 2015).

In the new materialist approach, an affective ecology is conjugated, after Spinoza, as an affirmative category of 'vibrancy', 'playfulness', and 'attunement', qualities that emerge anew, despite late industrialism's efforts to demolish them.[17] Carla Hustak and Natasha Myers, for instance, have conceptualized an 'affective ecology' as an extensive, distributed, and entangling sensorium wherein affinities are built to deliver pleasurable, playful, creative encounters between scientists and plants.[18] In this conception, the task at hand is to strategically 'amplify' vibrancy so as to strip ecology of its functionalist and hierarchical features and reimagine it as a playful flow that evidences both the traces of past inhabitation and possible responsive and responsible ways of co-cultivation with other species.[19] The anthropologist or artist is now graced with the analytical capacity to become a 'sensor',[20] to witness the emergence of a responsive milieu built by a convivial community of plants and bacterial organisms in communication with one another through chemical signalling, and to follow the traces of damaged life that unexpectedly blossom amid colonial and capitalist rubble. The point is to build an 'artful anthropology'[21] that seeks to demonstrate aesthetical and

17   See *Arts of Living on a Damaged Planet: Ghosts and Monsters of the Anthropocene*, ed. by Anna Lowenhaupt Tsing and others (Minneapolis: University of Minnesota Press, 2017), esp. Donna J. Haraway, 'Symbiogenesis, Sympoiesis, and Art Science Activisms for Staying with the Trouble', pp. M25–M50; Natasha Myers, 'Becoming Sensor in Sentient Worlds: A More-than-Natural History of a Black Oak Savannah', in *Between Matter and Method*, ed. by Gretchen Bakke and Marina Peterson (London: Routledge, 2017), pp. 73–96.

18   Carla Hustak and Natasha Myers, 'Involutionary Momentum: Affective Ecologies and the Sciences of Plant/Insect Encounters', *Differences*, 23.3 (2012), pp. 74–118 <https://doi.org/10.1215/10407391-1892907>.

19   Ibid., p. 79.

20   Myers, 'Becoming Sensor in Sentient Worlds', p. 76.

21   Ibid., p. 73.

practice-based modes of 'decolonial land care' that do not hinge on the destruction of the planet, but that illustrate 'arts of living on a damaged planet' under climate change.[22]

Tracing and thinking with battered yet tenacious indigenous worlds that centre interspecies relationality at their core; building a convergence between anthropology and the arts to arrive at an ecologically mindful aesthetics that raises the issue of responsibility and decolonial collaboration against 'mad-made' extinction exacerbated by the impending climate catastrophe — these ruminations interpret life as a vibrant 'ecological sensorium'.[23] Haraway, for instance, has recently proposed to tune research in to the generative and mutual 'capacity to respond' between humans and their co-inhabitants to stimulate reflection on collective and creative forms of communication that she calls 'worlding'.[24] Worlding is a reparative project that must include 'mourning [the] irreversible losses' that indigenous people have already been forced to endure under industrialist ecocide, but without necessarily ceasing the ongoing processes of making kin with the ecological features of the land.[25] Haraway highlights two cases of what she terms 'science art activism'.[26] The *Crochet Coral Reef* is a collaborative art project knitted in crochet by some eight thousand people across twenty-seven countries that reconstructs a coral reef ecosystem made of waste reel-to-reel tape, plastic bags and wraps, discarded vinyl, and other discarded material to showcase the interconnection between global warming, pollution, and extinction. For

---

22   *Arts of Living on a Damaged Planet*, ed. by Tsing and others.
23   Myers, 'Becoming Sensor in Sentient Worlds', p. 75.
24   Haraway, 'Symbiogenesis, Sympoiesis, and Art Science Activisms for Staying with the Trouble', pp. M38 and M25.
25   Ibid., p. M35.
26   Ibid., p. M33.

Haraway, the responsiveness that the project generates is an example of consciousness raising that cultivates an inter-species relationality based on mutual responsibility and care to counter industrialist destruction: 'we are all corals now'.[27] Similarly, the Ako Project, an artistic inventory of spiritual, ritualistic, and ecological features of the rich bio-diversity of Madagascar as understood and cared for by the Malagasy, provides a history of the damage done to terrain by colonial land grabbing, developmentalist extractivism, and failed humanitarian projects. For Haraway, affective ecology is a 'sensible materialism' that aesthetically invites attention to damaged local worlds responding to the imme-diate threat of extinction under climate change by engaging spiritual, ritualistic, and resistant local practices in an effort to protect highly distinctive ecological milieus and ancient knowledge systems.[28]

Against the habitual relegation of the cosmological realm to superstition and the ecological field to primordial engagement in rational approaches to politics, Dorothy Kwek and Robert Seyfert draw attention to those battles that illustrate, in their words, an affective and ecological *partition of the sensible*.[29] An affective ecology is after 'a more nuanced account of how human agencies are em-bedded within, constrained by, entangled with, and con-stituted by more-than-human others', partly to 'help us understand the full consequences and costs of what we imagine as "human" actions'.[30] Consider the 140-year legal

---

27   Ibid., p. M39.

28   Ibid., p. M45.

29   Dorothy H. B. Kwek and Robert Seyfert, 'Affect Matters: Strolling through Heterological Ecologies', *Public Culture*, 30.1 (2018), pp. 35–59 (p. 37) <https://doi.org/10.1215/08992363-4189155>; see also Jacques Rancière, *Dissensus: On Politics and Aesthetics* (London: Bloomsbury Publishing, 2010).

30   Ibid., p. 39.

battle fought by the Māori *iwi* (tribe) of Whanganui for the Whanganui River in New Zealand to be acknowledged as a living ancestor and accorded the same legal status as a human being by the Australian settler state. Or the legal battle in Uttarakhand, northern India, for the Ganges and Yamuna rivers to be recognized as legal entities.

While the focus on interspecies mutuality and vibrancy under the so-called man-made extinction is descriptively important within the larger context of decolonial land struggles in the era of climate change, this volume considers some of this work as an exercise in 'fascination with ecologically infused intimacies' which, according to Kath Weston, is a 'symptom — perhaps a sign, worthy of investigation in its own right'.[31] That is, the romantic gesture toward vibrant mutuality remains problematic from this more-than-human ecology perspective, for it both restores the 'ecological field' as a precolonial condition with which to counter colonial and capitalist degradation and projects researchers' ideals of wholesomeness and childlike innocence onto 'nature' and 'natives' as a way of brushing aside anxieties of contemporary planetary collapse. There is a conservative impulse in these accounts that hampers theoretical engagement with decolonial struggles and modern sites of eco-praxis occurring in worlds continuously and actively ravaged by the fourfold force of colonial occupation, genocidal annihilation, war, and capitalist extraction.

These problems were exemplified in the much-debated curatorial statement of the 16th Istanbul Biennial of 2018 that acknowledged both the necessity of ending the canonical Western division between nature and culture and the need for a transdisciplinary collaboration

---

31   Kath Weston, *Animate Planet: Making Visceral Sense of Living in a High-Tech Ecologically Damaged World* (Durham, NC: Duke University Press, 2017), p. 4.

between anthropology and the arts when studying the so-called Anthropocene.[32] The colonialist and primordialist underpinnings of the Biennial's curatorial statement, which considers the ethnographer and the artist as 'foreigners' who 'immerse' themselves in 'unknown societies' in order to attain a 'renewed exoticism', not only whitewashes the powerful decolonial critique emanating from within the discipline of anthropology against the roles of the researcher as a 'colonizer', an 'outsider', and an 'objective observer'. It also suffers from its argumentative grounding in the much-disputed and long-exhausted decolonial framework of Brazilian anthropologist Eduardo Viveiros de Castro, wherein Amazonian natives, as the epitomes of purity and wisdom, become the repository of the (white, heterosexual, cis-male) anthropologist's colonial and structuralist fantasies of fighting back against the Anthropocene.[33] Recent Amazonian ethnographies, which potentially have much to offer to discussions on decolonial land struggles and coalition-building, suffer from a similar kind of theoretical and aesthetical myopia that the curatorial statement embodies, where the invitation to 'decolonize thought'[34]

---

32   Nicolas Bourriaud, 'Curator's Statement', *Istanbul Foundation for Culture and Arts*, 2019 <https://bienal.iksv.org/en/16th-istanbul-biennial/curator-s-statement> [accessed 30 March 2022].

33   For exquisite critiques, see Lucas Bessire and David Bond, 'Ontological Anthropology and the Deferral of Critique', *American Ethnologist*, 41.3 (2014), pp. 440–56 <https://doi.org/10.1111/amet.12083>; David Graeber, 'Radical Alterity Is Just Another Way of Saying "Reality": A Reply to Eduardo Viveiros de Castro', *HAU: Journal of Ethnographic Theory*, 5.2 (2015), pp. 1–41 <https://doi.org/10.14318/hau5. 2.003>; Orin Starn, 'HERE COME THE ANTHROS (AGAIN): The Strange Marriage of Anthropology and Native America', *Cultural Anthropology*, 26.2 (2011), pp. 179–204 <https://doi.org/10.1111/j. 1548-1360.2011.01094.x>.

34   Compare Eduardo Kohn, *How Forests Think: Toward an Anthropology Beyond the Human* (Berkeley: University of California Press, 2013).

and 'provincialize reason' deliver seriously exoticizing political consequences that obfuscate the consideration of decolonial ecological programmes and praxis of modern horizons.[35] Recent anthropological works, for instance, prompt us to move beyond a mere acceptance of anthropological thinking as a transparent epistemological field and instead to undo its exoticizing methodological underpinnings.[36] Rather than delving deeper into the archives of structuralism with a relativist and ontological twist under the guise of decolonial thought and its reverberating curatorial aesthetics, this volume offers fresh insights into what happens to life as the effects and threat of organized mass violence continue to reverberate across species throughout war-torn worlds and their diasporas. The analytical eschewal of the constitutive spiral of mass violence in the Middle Eastern sites in which we work is an ethnographic, aesthetical, conceptual, and political life sentence. The Biennial's curatorial statement promotes an ecological sensitivity that callously ignores the violence of militarist extraction by war and genocide endured and pushed back by communities, an especially egregious aporia considering the exhibition's location in Turkey where war against the Kurds has been ongoing in the context of the state's denial of the Armenian genocide.

To put it differently, it is no coincidence that projects like the *Feral Atlas: The More-Than-Human Anthropocene*, which promotes the urgency of attending to the so-called

---

35   Umut Yıldırım, 'Resistant Breathing: Ruined and Decolonial Ecologies in a Middle Eastern Heritage Site', *Current Anthropology*, forthcoming.

36   Jafari Sinclaire Allen and Ryan Cecil Jobson, 'The Decolonizing Generation: (Race and) Theory in Anthropology since the Eighties', *Current Anthropology*, 57.2 (2016), pp. 129–48 <https://doi.org/10.1086/685502>; Ryan Cecil Jobson, 'The Case for Letting Anthropology Burn: Sociocultural Anthropology in 2019', *American Anthropologist*, 122.2 (2020), pp. 259–71 <https://doi.org/10.1111/aman.13398>.

Anthropocene as the ultimate form of political responsibility and as the motor force of intellectual and artistic
inquiry in the era of climate change, have found their way to
the Istanbul Biennial.[37] This interactive digital platform, a
five-year project of digital environmental humanities from
Stanford University Press curated by Anna Tsing, Jennifer
Deger, Alder Keleman Saxena, and Feifei Zhou, involves
one hundred artists, scientists, and anthropologists.[38] Led
by Tsing, who in 2020 was named one of the most powerful people in the artworld in *Art Review*'s 'Power 100', an
annual ranking of the most influential people in art, the
project develops further the central arguments of Tsing's
*The Mushroom at the End of the World: On the Possibility
of Life in Capitalist Ruin* and sets itself the task of commit-
ting 'more-than-human histories' to 'cultivate vital forms
of recognition and response to the urgent environmental
challenges of our times'.[39] Designed as an interactive, work-
in-progress digital document, the *Atlas* studies the unexpected ecological consequences of industrial infrastructures
such as plantations, shipping routes, factories, dams, power
stations, and drilling rigs. Species facing mass extinction
due to monocrop farming, viruses, and bacteria generated
by industrial plant and animal production sites, dumping
grounds for industrial waste, and life emerging anew amidst
capitalist destruction — all make their way into the *Atlas*.
Now faced with critiques of their earlier universalist,[40] ra-

---

37 'Feral Atlas Collective', *Istanbul Foundation for Culture and Arts*, 2019
    <https://bienal.iksv.org/en/bienal-artists/feral-atlas-collective> [ac-
    cessed 30 March 2022].

38 *Feral Atlas: The More-Than-Human Anthropocene*, ed. by Anna Lowen-
    haupt Tsing and others (Stanford University Press, 2021) <https://doi.
    org/10.21627/2020fa>.

39 Ibid.

40 Vansintjan, 'Going beyond the "Ecological Turn" in the Human-
    ities', *Entitle Blog – A Collaborative Writing Project on Political Ecol-*

cist,[41] and colonialist[42] constitution, the anthropologies of the Anthropocene have recently been revised to incorporate geographies and histories of genocide and colonialism into their framework and attend to the uneven ecological traces and effects of these oppressive systems that dominate landscapes with large industrial patches.[43] Yet still the revised framework's consideration of mass violence remains reductive: the violent processes of colonial occupation and extraction are taken on as a mere analytical issue of inclusivity, a move that diversifies the conceptual framework of the Anthropocene but does not radically alter it.

The point with this volume is not to lift up, buttress, or nuance the notion of the Anthropocene with an 'add Middle Eastern geographies and stir' approach. Instead, the reflections here aim to counter head-on the constitutive indifference to processes of racialization and geographical profiling that are embedded in the very notion of the Anthropocene, while at the same time being mindful of the epistemological violence of the terminological focus on vibrancy, radical alterity, and climactic urgency. Fine-tuning Gaston Gordillo's[44] proposal to understand colonial space as a negatively charged affective constellation that is enmeshed with rubbled objects and (we add) ecological

---

ogy, 2016 <https://entitleblog.org/2016/03/01/going-beyond-the-ecological-turn-in-the-humanities/> [accessed 26 July 2019].

41   Vergès, 'Racial Capitalocene'.

42   Zoe Todd, 'An Indigenous Feminist's Take on the Ontological Turn: "Ontology" Is Just Another Word for Colonialism', Journal of Historical Sociology, 29.1 (2016), pp. 4–22 <https://doi.org/10.1111/johs.12124>.

43   See Anna Lowenhaupt Tsing, Andrew S. Mathews, and Nils Bubandt, 'Patchy Anthropocene: Landscape Structure, Multispecies History, and the Retooling of Anthropology: An Introduction to Supplement 20', Current Anthropology, 60.S20 (2019), pp. S186–97 <https://doi.org/10.1086/703391>.

44   Gastón R. Gordillo, Rubble: The Afterlife of Destruction (Durham, NC: Duke University Press, 2014), p. 20.

debris that appear around the edges of destruction, the volume meditates on ecology's war-torn yet resistant affective movement in the Middle East. This is to arrive at war-torn ecologies.

WAR-TORN ECOLOGIES

In this volume, the will to challenge the structuring role of the imperialist and genocidal underpinnings of Eurocentric epistemologies in defining and constituting contemporary theories of affect is articulated under the rubric of war-torn ecologies. In undoing the violence that epistemological and aesthetical overreliance on white genealogies generates, this volume takes its lead from two works on critical human geography that focus on race in the US context. *War-torn Ecologies* proposes to interlace Middle Eastern ecologies with what Ruth Wilson Gilmore[45] has termed an 'abolitionist geography' and what Katherine McKittrick[46] refers to as 'demonic grounds'. Rather than forcing analysis into a continuous spiral of destruction, abolitionist geography seeks to free the 'still-to-be-achieved' work of emancipation from processes of 'hierarchy, dispossession, and exclusion'[47] intrinsic to colonial encroachment and imperialist violence. Taking raced structures of feeling to be constitutive of the bonding between human and environmental processes, Gilmore provides us with a conceptual toolkit for challenging normative perspectives in which territory and liberation are mutually exclusive terms to be alienated and then occupied by militarist technolo-

---

45   Ruth Wilson Gilmore, 'Abolition Geography and the Problem of Innocence', in *Futures of Black Radicalism*, ed. by Gaye Theresa Johnson and Alex Lubin (London: Verso, 2017), pp. 225–40.

46   Katherine McKittrick, *Demonic Grounds: Black Women and the Cartographies of Struggle* (Minneapolis: University of Minnesota Press, 2006).

47   Gilmore, 'Abolition Geography and the Problem of Innocence', p. 228.

gies such as 'sales, documents, or walls'.[48] A project not 'only by, for, or about Black people',[49] abolitionist geography embraces the political strategy of discussing raced sites of destruction together with praxis.

McKittrick's 'demonic grounds' is one such abolitionist geography. 'The built environment and the material landscape are sites that are intensely experiential and uneven, and deeply dependent on psychic, imaginary work',[50] McKittrick writes. In retracing the pathways of lost or trivialized knowledge in geographical canons, McKittrick shows how a seeming site of oppression can in fact be 'a terrain of political struggle'.[51] These demonic grounds not only spatially locate and push back against structures and patters of domination and exploitation that subordinate Black women's bodies, sexualities, subjectivities, and desires, they also provide a generative account of how Black imaginaries lie at the very core of the unfinished work of liberation and struggle over social space.

The present volume finds comradery in these works, as they furnish a set of concepts for understanding how ecology is an integral yet resistant part of ongoing militarist expansion, racism, and geographical debilitation. Accordingly, our works are influenced by recent anthropological accounts that bridge the gap between the otherwise disparate fields of materiality, affect, and war in the Middle East.[52] We learn from these accounts that imperialist and

---

48   Ibid., p. 238.

49   Ibid.

50   Ibid., p. 2.

51   Ibid., p. 8.

52   Salih Can Açıksöz, *Sacrificial Limbs: Masculinity, Disability, and Political Violence in Turkey* (Berkeley: University of California Press, 2019); Sophia Stamatopoulou-Robbins, *Waste Siege: The Life of Infrastructure in Palestine* (Stanford, CA: Stanford University Press, 2019); Kenneth MacLeish and Zoë H. Wool, 'US Military Burn

colonial (mis)management of military waste in the Middle East disturbs accounts of planetary connectedness and continuity under climate change by actively producing toxic landscapes and legacies of living. Kenneth MacLeish and Zoë Wool, for instance, show how the open-air burn pits on US bases into which the US military and contractor firms have been dumping waste in Iraq release toxic chemicals that have resulted in illnesses among US Iraq War veterans.[53] Sophia Stamatopoulou-Robbins similarly demonstrates how the environmentalist rescue work of 'saving the planet' frames and shapes the technocratic management of trash in Palestine as an issue of 'environmental peace building'[54] that not only enables claims made to the West Bank's environment by the Israeli state and international technocrats, but also covers up the actual wounds of the occupation inflicted by Israel. Moving the analytical lens away from the world of US veterans and decision-making technocrats, Kali Rubaii meditates on the 'toxic legacies' of the occupation of Iraq to show how military waste including bombs, bullets, chemical weaponry, open-air burn pits, and junkyards is not mere background to occupation but actively constitutes the landscape by turning cancer and congenital illness into ordinary occurrences.[55] Salih Can Açıksöz further illustrates that, in the context of the ongoing war in northern Kurdistan between the Turk-

Pits and the Politics of Health', *Medical Anthropology Quarterly Critical Care Blog*, 2018 <https://medanthroquarterly.org/critical-care/2018/08/us-military-burn-pits-and-the-politics-of-health/> [accessed 24 March 2022].

53   MacLeish and Wool, 'US Military Burn Pits and the Politics of Health'.

54   Stamatopoulou-Robbins, *Waste Siege*, p. 189.

55   Kali Rubaii, 'Birth Defects and the Toxic Legacy of War in Iraq', *Middle East Report*, 296 (Fall 2020) <https://merip.org/2020/10/birth-defects-and-the-toxic-legacy-of-war-in-iraq-296/> [accessed 12 November 2022].

ish state and the Kurdish movement organized around the Kurdistan Workers' Party (PKK) and given their function as the ultimate political symbol of sacrifice for the Turkish nation, disabled Turkish veterans returning home to Turkish cities linger affectively in the martial ecology of the mountains by physically embodying the visceral traces of a 'pastoral devastated by war and littered with ruins and military garbage'.[56] The affective state of 'being-on-the-mountains'[57] under war is a sensorial amalgamation of 'heightened perception and [a] sense of vulnerability'[58] for soldiers faced with impending lethal danger on the battlefield that lingers on into the post-return urban present as various affective states of conquest, unexpected shock, classed and gendered disappointment when their expectation of being politically crowned as war heroes falls flat.

The present volume attempts something more by thinking through ecological constellations from the perspective of human and more-than-human actors whose racialized and geographically regimented lives are interrupted and violated by *ongoing* ecocide, even after the sporadic spiral of mass violence briefly ends and the 'white man' leaves only to be replaced with incoming troops. *War-torn Ecologies* orients the reader into brown worlds where life is occupied, debilitated, and constituted by war, colonial ecocide, genocidal aftermaths, and genocide denialism; where life is routinely illegalized, rendered undocumentable, and unaccountable by sovereign states and their imperialist allies; where life is brimming with brown feelings of refusal, with a brown affective dramaturgy that illustrates ecological protraction and praxis amidst genocidal ruins, war rubble, and toxicity.

---

56   Açıksöz, *Sacrificial Limbs*, p. 21.
57   See chapter one in ibid., p. 15.
58   Ibid., p. 35.

AN-ARCHIC FRAGMENTS, AESTHETICAL
INTERVENTIONS

War-torn Ecologies creates an an-archic encounter between
anthropology and the arts with a critical perspective that
builds on recent work that casts doubt on the ostensibly
intrinsic 'goodness' of artistic practices. In her analysis
of the contemporary art world in Turkey and Germany,
Banu Karaca[59] has demonstrated how artistic production
serves as a violent medium of 'systematic forgetting',[60] a
smokescreen that enables settler states and their corporate allies to whitewash and deny the genocides, displacements, and dispossessions they themselves carry out. The
violent 'civilizing mission' intrinsic to the history of art
and its institutions generates common-sensical definitions
of citizenship while simultaneously contravening the self-
declared emancipatory power of art and its institutions.
Karaca encourages her readers to think through economic
dispossession and aesthetic absences and omissions in national art histories and collections.

Creative acts that expose and denounce the under-
lying connections between war profiteering, philanthropic
investment in the arts sector, imperialist processes of geographical occupation, as well as the institutional and curatorial strategies that omit such facts sow the seeds of war-
torn ecologies by debunking the myth that the art world in
contemporary global metropoles is somehow innocent of
centuries of colonial, slaving, extractivist, and warmongering accumulation. Consider the call of the *Décoloniser les
arts* initiative in France, which creates campaigns to expose
and denounce censorship and structural racism in French

---

59   Banu Karaca, *The National Frame: Art and State Violence in Turkey and
     Germany* (New York: Fordham University Press, 2021).
60   Ibid., p. 140.

artistic circles and institutions and carves out spaces of
action for the aesthetic recognition of Afrodescendant imaginaries, not as objects of tolerance that fulfil white fantasies of inclusivity and diversity for a better France, but
as wounded yet generative critical forces to be reckoned
with on their own terms. Consider the artistic and activist intervention that emerged in the wake of the MoMA
exhibition in New York, 'Theater of Operations: The Gulf
Wars 1991–2011', from November 2019 to early March
2020.[61] This massive assemblage featuring works by Iraqi
and Kuwaiti artists at home and in the diaspora who have
lived through US-manufactured occupations and two Gulf
wars was contested by a series of interventions that revealed the implication of two trustees of its institutional
affiliate, MoMA PS1, in private prisons, ICE detention
centres, private military contractors, and the arms trade
that had directly caused some of the destruction on public display at the exhibition. While some Arab artists were
denied entry to the US to attend the opening, others withdrew their works in protest or requested room to reorient
their works to expose the warmongering philanthropy that
is intrinsic to the art world. Consider *Decolonize This Place*,
an activist and artistic collaboration that germinated from
the Occupy Wall Street movement which seeks to fuel
struggles around 'indigeneity, Black liberation, free Palestine, global wage workers and de-gentrification',[62] and
Forensic Architecture's interventions in the Whitney Biennial in 2019. The latter exposed Whitney board member
Warren B. Kanders' ownership of the Safariland Group,

---

61   'Theater of Operations: The Gulf Wars 1991–2011', *The Museum of Mod-
      ern Art*, 2019 <https://www.moma.org/calendar/exhibitions/5084>
      [accessed 1 April 2022].

62   'Palestine', *Decolonize This Place*, 2020 <https://decolonizethisplace.
      org/palestine-1> [accessed 1 April 2022].

which manufactured tear gas to be used against migrants at the US–Mexico border and in the Gaza Strip in Palestine. When *Artforum*, one of the most powerful publications in the contemporary art world, published a letter by Ciarán Finlayson, Tobi Haslett, and Hannah Black titled 'The Tear Gas Biennial', which invited artists to withdraw their work from the Biennial in protest, ongoing rallying in alternative platforms such as *Hyperallergic* managed to reach a wider audience. While *Decolonize This Place* endorsed staffers' demand for the resignation of the board member, *Forensic Architecture*, before finally withdrawing from the Biennial, ignited the scene with a declaration that their contribution would consist of a video focusing on the tear gas produced by the company. As another example of protest art, consider Hito Steyerl's lecture performance 'Is the Museum a Battlefield?' where she explores the linkage between corporate sponsorship and warmongering in the context of the war between the Kurdish movement organized around the PKK and the Turkish state. The video work documents her journey of discovery of the fact that the Turkish machine-gun bullet that killed her friend Andrea Wolf in 1998 had been manufactured by Lockheed Martin, which was a sponsor of the 13th Istanbul Biennial where she delivered her work, and the patron of her exhibition at the Art Institute of Chicago. With a similar twist, Steyerl recently staged a performance at the Maxim Gorki Theatre in Berlin in 2019 requesting German state-run art institutions to exclude her work from their portfolio of 'external cultural diplomacy' until Germany recognizes the Turkish invasion of Kurdish areas in northeast Syria. Consider the 2019 performative intervention by the collective BP or Not BP? in which three hundred and fifty participants roamed the British Museum in protest of the mass-scale exhibition 'I Am Ashburnipal, King of the World, King of Assyria' in 2019, which contained many artefacts looted from what is now Iraq and whose primary sponsor was the British oil and gas company BP. The BP or Not BP? crew staged another intervention in 2019 by occupying the British Museum with a massive prop of the Trojan Horse in protest of BP's sponsorship of the exhibit 'Troy: Myth and Reality'. The performative work raised concerns about the ecological devastation caused by BP's work on the Trans-Anatolian Pipeline, a major gas transport line running across Turkey that passes from the site of ancient Troy.

While aesthetical interventions that showcase the militarist logic and investment inherent in the art-washing of mass violence buttress the notion of war-torn ecologies, this volume shifts the lens to think together with conceptual works that foment endurance and resistance in war-torn worlds and re-root ruptures by resisting erasure.

In 'Mulberry Affects', my own work explores the ruderal mulberry trees that line the shores of the Tigris River in the city of Amed, the informal capital of Greater Kurdistan, the Armenian name of which was and is Dikranagerd. Mulberry trees were no mere decorative detail set against the enormity of this ancient city and the surrounding destroyed villages but rather an-archic fragments of the genocidal erasure of Armenians, as well as Syriacs since the anti-Christian pogroms of 1895 and the still ongoing war between the Turkish state and the Kurdish movement organized around the PKK. By paying attention to the archival erasure of Armenian nativity to the land and the resistant roots of centenarian mulberry trees that are scattered across the Tigris riverbank, I attempt to raise questions around supposedly 'abandoned' ecological sites.

With her video work 'Who's Afraid of Ideology?' artist Marwa Arsanios creates an-archic fragments of occupation in Rojava made of wild medicinal plants, fig trees

planted by the Syrian regime, Kurdish guerrillas, and female farmers in the Jinwar commune, literally, the 'place
of women', a village built on land reappropriated for the
exclusive use of women in Rojava. Self-defence here is
ongoing daily work that is deeply enmeshed in ecology.
Self-defence is a medicinal-plant manifesto; a mundane
praxis of land and community care resisting the threat of
militarist offence and colonial occupation.

Kali Rubaii invites her readers to ethnographically
sense a war-torn landscape of 'toxic legacy' in Iraq, where
the spectacular and the ordinary merge to evidence an ecological constellation constituted by the military rubble of
the Second Gulf War (2003); where toxic war materials
occupy bodies with premature death, cancer, and congenital illness; where war chemicals infiltrate the atmosphere,
water, and soil, and lodge in people's dreams and experiences as ghosts and spiritual entities such as jinns.

An-archic fragments emerge in the artistic work of
Nadine Hattom as she builds a new aesthetical world on
the broken shell and fragmented memories of the occupation of her family home in Iraq during the Iran–Iraq
War (1980–88) and the First Gulf War (1990–99) with
'Shadows', a series of ten digitally modified photographs
from the US Department of Defense Operation Iraqi Freedom archive. Hattom builds an affective montage between
the desert landscape of her homeland and the 'sandy dunes'
that she discovers by accident in an ancient black forest
in her exilic new home in Germany that serve as a military training field for American troops before they are
deployed to Iraq. Sand is her affective association with the
flora, fauna, earth, and sky of her homeland, the ecological
elements and the brown palette that exert a war-torn yet
enduring force that haunts the artist even when she is building new homes elsewhere.

In South Lebanon, Munira Khayyat takes us to an agricultural world where herders farm under a military chokehold supervised by Israeli patrols and occasionally have to follow their goats into a grey zone that lies between a fence separating Lebanon and Israel and the 'Blue Line' of the United Nations-designated frontier. Technologies of death are somewhat thwarted by the lively, resistant, multi-species ecologies of the borderland. Tricking mines is by no means an easy art or an accurate science, and the threat of death-in-livelihood is ever-present.

Collectively, our encounters as anthropologists and artists inspires us to build an ecologically-infused perspective on mass violence. We do this by embracing dissident forms of anthropological and artistic research that contest commonsensical narratives of geopolitical supremacy, militarist normalcy, and climatic urgency. We embrace remembrance, endurance, and praxis. We breathe steadfastly against war.

Ours is the gesture of reclaiming brown breath.

Mulberry Affects
Ecology, Memory, and Aesthetics on the Shores of the Tigris River in the Wake of Genocide
UMUT YILDIRIM

PRELUDE: IN THE SHADOWS

Imagine an ancient Middle Eastern city whose two popular names have been illegalized by a sovereign state. Disregard for aspects of the toponymical and demographic past is commonplace in colonialist and nationalist place naming practices, and the official name for the city of Diyarbakır in Turkey's Kurdistan, where I have been conducting fieldwork since 2004, is no exception. Suffice it to say that this official toponomy was the genocidal result of academic, bureaucratic, demographic, and military Turkification efforts on the part of government administrators and experts, as evidenced by the coining of the name by Turkish Republican elite in 1937.[1] In the province of Diyarbekir, rule had

---

1   See Kerem Öktem, 'Incorporating the Time and Space of the Ethnic "Other": Nationalism and Space in Southeast Turkey in the Nineteenth and Twentieth Centuries', *Nations and Nationalism*, 10.4 (2004), pp. 559–78 <https://doi.org/10.1111/j.1354-5078.2004.00182.x>.

been imposed through a series of pogroms, displacements, dispossessions, and resettlements that intensified in the nineteenth century and culminated in the 1915 genocide of Armenians by the Ottoman state.[2] Although the Republic's denialist naming practices effectively erased both Kurds' and non-Muslim non-Turkish peoples' existence and the violence Ottoman-cum-Republican elites and their various collaborators had perpetrated against them from the official map,[3] the toponomy of Diyarbakır continued to be haunted by its Armenian and Kurdish heritage.[4] The Western Armenian name of 'Dikranagerd' used during the Ottoman

---

2   Fuat Dündar, *İttihat Ve Terakki'nin Müslümanları İskan Politikasi (1913–1918)* (Istanbul: İletişim Yayınları, 2001); Fuat Dündar, *Modern Türkiye'nin Şifresi: İttihat Ve Terakki'nin Ethnisite Mühendisliği, 1913–1918* (Istanbul: İletişim Yayınları, 2008); *Armenian Tigranakert/Diarbekir and Edessa/Urfa*, ed. by Richard G. Hovannisian (Costa Mesa, CA: Mazda Publishers, 2006); Joost Jongerden, *The Settlement Issue in Turkey and the Kurds: An Analysis of Spatial Policies, Modernity and War* (Leiden: Brill, 2007); Joost Jongerden, 'Elite Encounters of a Violent Kind: Milli İbrahim Paşa, Ziya Gökalp and Political Struggle in Diyarbekir at the Turn of the 20th Century', in *Social Relations in Ottoman Diyarbekir, 1870-1915*, ed. by Joost Jongerden and Jelle Verheij (Leiden: Brill, 2012), pp. 55–84; Raymond Kévorkian, *Le Génocide des Arméniens* (Paris: Odile Jacob, 2006); Raymond Kévorkian and Paul Paboudjian, *Ermeniler: 1915 Öncesinde Osmanlı İmparatorluğu'nda*, trans. by Mayda Saris (Istanbul: Aras Yayıncılık, 2012); Vahé Tachjian, *Daily Life in the Abyss: Genocide Diaries, 1915–1918* (Oxford: Berghahn Books, 2017); Uğur Ümit Üngör, *The Making of Modern Turkey: Nation and State in Eastern Anatolia, 1913–1950* (Oxford: Oxford University Press, 2011); Uğur Ümit Üngör and Mehmet Polatel, *Confiscation and Destruction: The Young Turk Seizure of Armenian Property* (London: Bloomsbury Academic, 2011); Veli Yadırgı, *The Political Economy of the Kurds of Turkey: From the Ottoman Empire to the Turkish Republic* (Cambridge: Cambridge University Press, 2017).

3   *Armenian Tigranakert/Diarbekir and Edessa/*Urfa, ed. by Hovannisian; Talin Suciyan, *The Armenians in Modern Turkey: Post-Genocide Society, Politics and History* (London: I.B. Tauris, 2016).

4   Adnan Çelik and Namık Kemal Dinç, *Yüz Yıllık Ah! Toplumsal Hafızanın İzinde: 1915 Diyarbakır* (İstanbul: İsmail Beşikçi Vakfı, 2015); Joost Jongerden, *The Settlement Issue in Turkey and the Kurds: An Analysis of Spatial Policies, Modernity and War* (Leiden: Brill, 2007); Umut Yıldırım, 'Space, Loss and Resistance: A Haunted Pool-Map in South-

period was retained by the Armenian diaspora and in the
Soviet Socialist Republic of Armenia, while the Kurdish
name of 'Amed', which references the Kurdish movement's
informal capital of Kurdistan, gained popularity in the
1990s during the escalating guerrilla war between the Kurdistan Worker's Party (*Partîya Karkerên Kurdistanê*, PKK)
and successive Turkish governments.[5] As a contested toponymy, the name 'Diyarbakır' is a total eclipse. It structures
the denialist post-genocide present by obscuring the nested
yet layered nativity of Christians and non-Turkish Muslims
to the land. In current debates over ancestral custodian-
ship, land, and property claims, such eclipsing toponymy
suggests that fieldwork in this genocidal geography of war
should begin in the shadows by using an analytical radar
attuned to the processes of redaction.

Not only has the dramatic and sedimented history of
this genocidal city of seasoned rebellion piqued my concerns around an-archic justice, but the association of its
ancient urban agricultural plots with 'lungs' has inspired my
imagination to propose the idea of eco-redaction as an aesthetic manoeuvre for thinking with erasure so as to uncover
ecological clusters of destruction and transformation.[6] In
acknowledging Marc Nichanian's observation that attempt-
ing to comprehend the genocide through reason, fact, and
closure is a doomed endeavour predicated on its own collapse,[7] I ask a number of pointed theoretical, methodo-

Eastern Turkey', *Anthropological Theory*, 19.4 (2019), pp. 440–469.
<https://doi.org/10.1177/1463499618783130>.

5   Although the city is popularly named Dikranagerd among Armenians,
     the precise location of Dikranagerd remains unknown. See *Armenian
     Tigranakert/Diarbekir and Edessa/Urfa*, ed. by Hovannisian.

6   Umut Yıldırım, 'Resistant Breathing: Ruined and Decolonial Ecologies
     in a Middle Eastern Heritage Site', *Current Anthropology*, forthcoming.

7   Marc Nichanian, *The Historiographic Perversion*, trans. by Gil Anidjar
     (New York: Columbia University Press, 2009).

logical, and empirical questions. How can the Armenian genocide be considered in terms of its ecological roots and remnants? How can we acknowledge the layered processes of destruction while also accounting for the resurgence of multispecies life in war-torn geographies shaped by geno-cidal erasure and ongoing genocide denialism?

Here, I pay attention to centenarian mulberry trees growing along the shores of the Tigris River, together with their younger companions scattered across perished sites, that have survived more than a hundred years of genocidal massacre and solitude and that still resist destruction by sporadic yet ongoing military sieges through low intensity war. Reading against the narrative arc of the Turkish state's sovereign archive, which continues to deny that the Arme-nian genocide ever occurred, could centenarian mulberry trees on the Tigris riverbank be conceptualized as an-archic archives, with the potential to literally and affectively root Christian nativity to land and counter settler denialism?

In underscoring sediments of violence as they have accumulated along the shores of the Tigris River, my in-tention is not to flatten out the complex layering of claims over what constitutes 'settling' and 'indigeneity' in Diyar-bakır. Nuance in the question of commensurability over ancestral claims to land is particularly important given that some of the Muslims of various backgrounds and ethnici-ties who participated in the 1895 anti-Christian pogroms and the Armenian genocide were also native to the land. Historians and historical anthropologists have been attend-ing to such complex, contested, and violently traversed layering. Moreover, two recent ethnographic works are par-ticularly important to note here as they attend to such intra-communal relations and tensions in the genocidal wake. In their recent book, *The Century-Old Curse*, Adnan Çe-lik and Namık Kemal Dinç show, for instance, that while

villages, cities, landmarks, rivers, and provinces throughout northern Mesopotamia, particularly in Diyarbakır, have
taken on almost mythical status as sites of scarred longing
and ancestral pain within Armenian collective intergener-
ational memory, for Kurds, they have become sites that materialize Armenians' curses against Muslim perpetrators.[8]
The writers show how, in the imaginary and vernacular of
rural Kurds in Diyarbakır, Armenian curses were absorbed
by those geological sites where massacres occurred beginning in the late nineteenth century, including wells, dens,
caves, gorges, and streams. Çelik and Dinç argue that this
morphing of the curse into geological forms points to rural
Kurds' self-reflexivity vis-à-vis their ancestors' crimes in the
genocidal past. Indeed, the Kurds themselves have suffered
under the colonial rule of the Turkish state and have curses
of their own marked on the landscape to be redirected to
colonialists and their collaborators who orchestrated anti-
Kurdish pogroms. My point here, though, is not to force
equanimity on intercommunal convergences, tensions, and
conflicts between Muslims and Christians. Here, I draw on
Zerrin Özlem Biner's notion of 'ruined heritage' in which
a repertoire of intersecting temporalities of ongoing state
violence and dispossession in the aftermath of genocidal
expropriation excites business interests and causes intra-
communal conflict in the neighbouring multi-ethnic city
of Mardin.[9] Bereft of historical memory, heritage becomes
the conduit of an illusory existence, masking a continuum
of destruction that further conditions legal and intracom-
munal conflicts over already expropriated lands.

---

8   Adnan Çelik and Namık Kemal Dinç , *Yüz Yıllık Ah! Toplumsal Hafıza-*
     nın İzinde: 1915 Diyarbekir (İstanbul: İsmail Beşikçi Vakfı, 2015), p. 17.
9   Zerrin Özlem Biner, *States of Dispossession: Violence and Precarious Co-*
     existence in Southeast Turkey (Philadelphia: University of Pennsylvania
     Press, 2020), p. 42.

Hence, I propose here a methodological approach
that is purposefully humble in its emphasis on incommensurable and tension-aware forms of political convergence
against Turkish state-sovereign violence, rather than an
exhaustive chronicling of historical claims. If bifurcated
approaches to settler colonialism that neatly and statically
partition the world into settlers and natives are mistaken,
so too is a naïve equivalence between Kurdish and Armenian understandings of colonialism and emergent decolonial visions and paradigms. The advantage of centring
more-than-human life conceptually within Armenian resurgent politics is that it enables us to reckon with the
genocidal constitution and colonial management of supposedly feral, 'abandoned' ecological sites. Today's centenarian mulberry trees are literal and affective roots resisting
the erasure, confiscation, and reappropriation of ecological
life by colonial paradigms that have partitioned the world
between Turkish sites of developmentalist zeal and heavily
militarized Kurdish ancestral lands. Today's centenarians
along the shores of the Tigris River open an imaginative
horizon against genocide denialism by centring on more-
than-human lives as an-archic indexes of the anti-Christian
pogroms of 1895 that culminated in the genocide. An-
archy here means that 'abandonment', in its ecological
form, should be explored rather than assumed.

AN-ARCHY IN THE ARCHIVE

Using an an-archic perspective, on the one hand I propose how considering omissions in Ottoman and Turkish
archives constitutes the genocidal aftermath of the anti-
Christian pogroms of 1895, which culminated in the Armenian genocide by obstructing a space for its reckoning, and
thus enabling and recycling genocide denialism. On the

other hand, I propose how ecological resurgence pushes back against the logocentric hold of these archives. My attention here turns to Jacques Derrida, who by studying the etymological roots of the concept of archive drew a connection between the official prints of history, epistemic of rule, and structures of memory.[10] The Greek word *arkhē*, he notes, means both beginning and command, and links creation stories to government and law. Derrida informs us that the *arkheion*, or the archive, was originally 'a house, a domicile, an address', which was the residence of 'the superior magistrates, the archons, the commanding officers'.[11] Originally, archons and magistrates governed these archives, maintaining the epistemic, legal, and affective parameters of homeliness for rights-bearing citizens, and providing franchises and entitlements to the privileged.

Violence is an integral part of this archival homemaking. As Derrida takes a pass at Freudian psychoanalysis, he entangles the Freudian primal drive toward aggression and elimination embodied in the death drive with an 'archive destroying'[12] that provokes a collective amnesia by annihilating memory. Derrida bypasses the theoretical bottleneck of sovereign factuality that had jammed archival inquiries with problems they had created themselves in the first place. While the sovereign archons select, classify, order, and govern facts that build the house of citizenship, they also feverishly burn the house, so to speak, by erasing facts in order to escape responsibility for past atrocities, as well as future mass violence. It is, he notes, 'in this house arrest, that archives take place'.[13]

---

10   Jacques Derrida, *Archive Fever: A Freudian Impression*. (Chicago: University of Chicago Press, 1996).

11   Ibid., p. 9.

12   Ibid., p. 14.

13   Ibid., p. 10.

Recently, Jodi Byrd analyzed the sovereign archive in a critical way that went beyond Derrida — that is, beyond the written word, demonstrating that archival destruction does not necessarily lead to passive forgetfulness and amnesia, but rather to an active dissociation from facts unsuitable for the maintenance of sovereignty, or 'agnosia of colonialism'.[14] At its core, colonial agnosia reproduces archival destruction socially and affectively in the present by suspending issues around historical culpability and everyday complicity with such destruction. An agnosia about colonialism refers to the affective preference of staying in the dark about archival destruction. It is a socially and historically structured psychic investment in remaining ignorant of sovereign mass violence and its pulsing effects in the present. It is the disavowal, especially, of right-bearing citizens of sovereign and racial privilege, who invest in their own failure to comprehend mass violence as an ongoing relation that shapes political imagination and action within the constraints of sovereign facts. This type of investment prevents those who benefit most from colonialism from taking responsibility for the violence it perpetrates. Colonial agnosia is culpability and complicity historicized and temporalized.

Bringing Byrd's elaborations on active dissociation to the ecological realm, I revisit the Greek root of the word archive, *arkhē*, which means 'beginning, foundation, first place', and derives from the verb *arkhō*, meaning 'to begin, rule, govern'. In tune with methodologies that re-route the Greek root as an-archy,[15] I hope to foreground more-than-

---

14   Jodi Byrd, 'Silence Will Fall: The Cultural Politics of Colonial Agnosia' (unpublished manuscript, n. d.).

15   See Simon Critchley, *Infinitely Demanding: Ethics of Commitment, Politics of Resistance* (London: Verso, 2014); Jacques Rancière, 'Ten Theses on Politics', *Theory & Event*, 5.3 (2001); Simon Springer, *The Anarchist*

human life as a way of unsettling a sovereign perceptual design that renders massacres sites unthinkable and unrecognizable by denying the historical significance of genocidal processes, and thus naturalizing the 'genocidal will'[16] that is embedded in official Ottoman and Turkish archives. This perceptual design reproduces the ecological parameters of the present-day Turkish order, including its supposedly feral, wild, abandoned sites. Turning this archival perceptual design into a problematic, the an-archic perspective seeks to forge an affinity between archival omissions and ecological resurgence in officially denied or unrecognized massacre sites by paying close attention to the more-than-human life that emerges despite the odds from such sites, and the land claims that such resurgence might complicate.

Here, I follow Lerna Ekmekçioğlu's lead in mobilizing an imaginative approach to restoring Armenian presence and visibility to land that would allow a transition from the denialist present in Turkey to a 'utopian era' of Armenian self-possession.[17] For Ekmekçioğlu, in this imaginative utopian era, concrete naming practices, educational interventions, and commemorative efforts that go beyond a metaphorical de-linking from Turkish 'institutional, intellectual, and political barriers to acknowledgement' can restore Armenian nativity to the land.[18] As a political (and religious) minority scholar from Turkey well aware of, and

---

Roots of Geography: Toward Spatial Emancipation (Minneapolis: University of Minnesota Press, 2016); Facundo Vega, 'On Bad Weather: Heidegger, Arendt, and Political Beginnings', in *Weathering: Ecologies of Exposure*, ed. by Christoph F. E. Holzhey and Arnd Wedemeyer, Cultural Inquiry, 17 (Berlin: ICI Berlin Press, 2020), pp. 227–43 <https://doi.org/10.37050/ci-17_11>.

16 Nichanian, *The Historiographic Perversion*.

17 Lerna Ekmekçioğlu, 'Of Dark Pasts and Pipe Dreams: The Turkish University', *YILLIK: Annual of Istanbul Studies*, 3 (2021), pp. 185–93 <https://doi.org/10.53979/yillik.2021.12>.

18 Ibid., p. 193.

at times complicit with, settlers' 'moves to innocence' that
serve to assuage settler guilt in repatriation processes without working to redress the harm done to indigenous ways
and forms of life,[19] I follow Ekmekçioğlu's lead by envision-
ing an an-archic approach that contributes to utopian re-
storative projects centred on the repatriation of Armenian
land and life. The centenarian mulberry trees scattered
around the Tigris riverbank today are rooted in the memory of diasporic Armenians as commemorative lives index-
ing homeliness as well as destruction. Like 'living-dead
trees',[20] the resistant roots of the mulberry fold the past
into the present by an-archically sparking the imagination
to consider perpetual grief, anger, and the drive for self-
possession outside the deathly and denialist confines of
state-sovereign archives. An-archy is ecology historicized,
aestheticized, and thus, politicized, and its modus oper-
andi is eco-redaction.

ECO-REDACTION AS METHOD

My methodology in tackling this issue is eco-redaction.
After Christina Sharpe, I move beyond conventional dis-
ciplinary notions of archival factuality in the wake of Transatlantic slave trade. In conversation with Black feminist
scholarship, particularly that of Saidiya Hartman, and abolitionist through and through, Sharpe's project develops
new methodologies going beyond archival eradications
that castrate slave's lives and experience on the ship and

---

19   Eve Tuck and K. Wayne Yang, 'Decolonization Is Not a Metaphor',
     Decolonization: Indigeneity, Education & Society, 1.1 (8 September
     2012) <https://jps.library.utoronto.ca/index.php/des/article/view/
     18630> [accessed 12 November 2022].
20   See Aylin Vartanyan Dilaver, 'From Longing to Belong to Shaping the
     Longing: Dwelling with Armenian Women in Istanbul' (PhD diss.,
     European Graduate School, forthcoming).

beyond. Sharpe's aim is to abolish the very conceptual and archival framework that is constituted and pervaded by the anti-Black apparatus and racist logic in North America, one that forces Black researchers to obey terms and analytics that precondition their own decimation. 'We must become undisciplined', she writes.[21] In thinking with 'this pain of and in the archive', Sharpe claims and mobilizes the undisciplined force of imagination, not to 'make sense of [archival] silences, absences, and modes of dis/appearance', but to generate a processual ethics of radical care in the present and into the future against 'state-imposed regimes of surveillance'.[22] To this end, Sharpe theorizes 'wake work' as a methodology that stays on the side of the dead with a sensitivity toward the work of grief in building political aesthetics. Laced with manoeuvres of 'annotation' and 'redaction', wake work moves attention 'toward reading and seeing something in excess of what is caught in the frame; towards seeing something beyond visuality'.[23]

Now, I am aware of the risks of appropriating radical Black feminist theorizing for use in Middle Eastern contexts. Such a move would not only flatten the relational, ontological, and spiritual aspects of Black endurance and praxis, but it would also eclipse the particular structuring of effects and affects that underwrite histories of mass violence and genocide denialism in Turkey. In turning to Sharpe, my intention is more circumspect: I engage in archival wake work with the aim of mobilizing the resurgent power of an imagination that refrains from approximating the lived experience of Armenian life so as to produce a co-

---

21   Christina Sharpe, *In the Wake: On Blackness and Being* (Durham, NC: Duke University Press, 2016) <https://doi.org/10.1215/9780822373452>, p. 13.

22   Ibid., pp. 18, 12, and 20.

23   Ibid., p. 117.

herent, hopeful, or 'civilized' corrective to settler archives.
My point is not to detoxify an already toxic archive, but
to place the conditions that reproduce the impossibility of
generating historical facts of the genocide under a magni-
fying glass, and in so doing, carve out spaces in which to
understand 'abandoned sites' otherwise. Centenarian mulberries scattered across the Tigris' shores today contradict
state-sovereign assumptions that all is in order, and that
peaceful order has been guaranteed. Mulberries enable us
to take a closer look at the cracks in the cloak of state
sovereignty, bringing forth a tension between official documents of history and their faltering ecological grounds.

Here I toy with the idea of eco-redaction as a way to
think of ecological sites as media works that generate an
aesthetic and affective interface that is caught in the long
movement between destruction and resurgence. I embrace
the idea of eco-redaction as 'a counter to abandonment,
another effort to try to look, to try to really see'.[24] Such
'noticing'[25] means paying attention to mutant,[26] ruderal,[27]
and unexpected[28] ecologies that emerge at the rough edges
of colonial milieus and environmental histories. Rather
than romanticizing a pristine 'outside' of settler colonialism as a model for alternative modes of endurance with
an ontological twist, eco-redaction engages in 'edge think-

---

24   Ibid.
25   Anna Lowenhaupt Tsing, *The Mushroom at the End of the World: On
     the Possibility of Life in Capitalist Ruins* (Princeton, NJ: Princeton
     University Press, 2015).
26   Joseph Masco, 'Mutant Ecologies: Radioactive Life in Post–Cold War
     New Mexico', *Cultural Anthropology*, 19.4 (2004), pp. 517–50 <https:
     //doi.org/10.1525/can.2004.19.4.517>.
27   Bettina Stoetzer, 'Ruderal Ecologies: Rethinking Nature, Migration,
     and the Urban Landscape in Berlin', *Cultural Anthropology*, 33.2
     (2018), pp. 295–323 <https://doi.org/10.14506/ca33.2.09>.
28   Gastón R. Gordillo, *Rubble: The Afterlife of Destruction* (Durham, NC:
     Duke University Press, 2014).

ing', in which researchers encounter mutable ecological elements at the archival and on-the-ground edges of destruction. Eco-redaction, as I employ it here, entails the use of photographic images, texts, and zines to create a montage of 'critical fabulations' after Hartman as well as feelings designed to amplify the dissonant ways in which ecology has been pushed out of the order of a dignified life and reduced to background effect (see figures 1 to 6).

FEELING IN THE BLANKS

My conversations with the city's few remaining Syriac Christians and with a diasporic Diyarbakırite Armenian family whose ancestors had owned plots of land on either side of the Tigris River, most notably in the now-destroyed village of Qeterbel, had taught me to consider the affective dimension of the Tigris riverbanks. After several years of research in state archives and among derivative secondary sources in the hopes of establishing Armenian and Syriac ownership and/or cultivation of plots in and around the Hewsel Gardens before and after the Armenian genocide, and faced with the absence of documentary evidence in these archives, I came to realize that the archive is itself a logocentric chokehold; an imposing abstraction in need of further conceptualization.[29]

---

29   See Meltem Ahıska, 'Occidentalism and Registers of Truth: The Polit-
     ics of Archives in Turkey', *New Perspectives on Turkey*, 34 (2006), pp. 9–
     29 <https://doi.org/10.1017/S0896634600004350>; Ekmekçioğlu,
     Recovering Armenia: The Limits of Belonging in Post-Genocide Turkey
     (Stanford, CA: Stanford University Press, 2016); Yael Navaro, 'The
     Aftermath of Mass Violence: A Negative Methodology', *Annual Review
     of Anthropology*, 49.1 (2020), pp. 161–73 <https://doi.org/10.1146/
     annurev-anthro-010220-075549>; Marc Nichanian, *Writers of Disas-
     ter: Armenian Literature in the Twentieth Century* (Princeton: Taderon,
     2002); Nichanian, *The Historiographic Perversion*; Suciyan, *The Arme-
     nians in Modern Turkey*.

I sift through the pages of *A Mulberry Tree in Hewsel Gardens*,[30] a political memoir in the form of an interview between two Kurdish men from different generations, both of whom have served prison time as a result of their affiliations with Kurdish decolonization. The introduction to the memoir, written by the famous Kurdish novelist Mehmed Uzun, transforms the mulberry tree into the ecological counterpart to the old Kurdish intellectual, Canip Yıldırım,[31] about whom the memoir is written. In Uzun's hands, the tree becomes a witness to Kurdish intellectuals' struggle to give life dignity and meaning. It compels testimony: to the violence of the Ottoman and Turkish states since the turn of the twentieth century; to the long and riotous history of Kurdish political organizing; first to the presence, and then to the displacement and erasure of non-Turkish and non-Muslim communities of the city of Diyarbakır. The memoir is part of the trend of oral history in Turkey in early 2000s, where the Armenian genocide denied by official Turkish state discourse and the state archives that support it becomes a fact that builds methodologically on the differentially situated living memory of Armenian and Kurdish elders. In this literature, the Armenian genocide becomes a 'counter-hegemonic' fact regenerated as political memoir.[32] At one point in the memoir, Yıldırım narrates stories about his Armenian and Syriac neighbours who were skilled silk weavers. This brief pause acknowledging *en passant* Armenian and Syriac nativity to the land

---

30 Orhan Miroğlu, *Hevsel Bahçesinde Bir Dut Ağacı: Mehmet Uzun'un Sunuşuyla Canip Yıldırım'la Söyleşi* (Istanbul: Everest Yayınları, 2010).

31 No relation to the author.

32 Adnan Çelik and Ergin Öpengin, 'The Armenian Genocide in the Kurdish Novel: Restructuring Identity through Collective Memory', *European Journal of Turkish Studies. Social Sciences on Contemporary Turkey*, 2016, p. 2 <https://doi.org/10.4000/ejts.5291>.

allows me to 'notice'[33] the importance of mulberry trees for Kurdistan's now annihilated or forcibly displaced Christian peasants, farmers, and silk manufacturers.

While digitally accessible state archives demonstrate the important role that mulberry tree and endemic silkworm cultivation played in Ottoman Diyarbekir prior to 1915, evidence on the durable effects of the loss of expertise in mulberry cultivation, as well as in silk processing and weaving immediately following the annihilation of the Christian silk masters and the confiscation of silk factories and mulberry orchards is scarce. While Turkish secondary sources based on state archives generally tie the decrease in silk production and mulberry orchards to global events, such as World War I and the economic crisis of 1929/1930,[34] and later, in the 1990s and mid-2010s, to the 'terrorism' of the PKK,[35] new work comparing district-level agricultural production and population data from the pre- and post-World War I periods suggests that, in addition to other agricultural crops under study, the 90 percent decline in the Ottoman/Turkish silk industry between 1907 and 1936 may have been a consequence of Armenian human capital loss in the genocide.[36] Following the genocide, Armenian existence all but vanished along the shores

---

33 Tsing, *The Mushroom at the End of the World*.

34 Tahir Öğüt and Çiğdem Çadırcı, 'Cumhuriyet Dönemine Geçiş Sürecinde Diyarbakır'da İktisadi-Mali ve Sosyal Yapı', *Gazi Akademik Bakış*, 7.13 (2013), pp. 141–70 (p. 154).

35 Compare Zafer Başkaya, 'Diyarbakır İli İpekböcekçiliğinin Türkiye'de Yeri ve Mekansal Analizi' [The Place and Spatial Analysis of Sericulture in Diyarbakir Province of Turkey], in *Uluslararası Diyarbakır Sempozyumu*, ed. by Ufuk Bircan and others (Diyarbakır: T. C. Diyarbakır Valiliği Kültür Sanat Yayınları, 2017), XVIII, pp. 2191–2217 (p. 2214).

36 See Ayça Akarçay, Nurhan Davutyan, and Sezgin Polat, *Economic Consequences of Demographic Engineering: Turkey and WWI* (Rochester, NY: Social Science Research Network, 15 April 2021), pp. 9 and 12 <https://doi.org/10.2139/ssrn.3828518>.

of the Tigris River and that the number of Diyarbakır's
mulberry trees and orchards decreased precipitously.

The absence of a formal archive that might document chronological Christian ownership of the orchards
was unsurprising: the archives of the Ottoman Committee of Union and Progress, which orchestrated the genocide, were destroyed soon after 1915, and the archives of
the succeeding Turkish state, which officially denies the
genocide, 'have very little to say, if anything at all' on the
matter.[37] Furthermore, a series of legal and administrative
manoeuvres enabling the confiscation and expropriation
of 'abandoned' property by the state, including a series
of abandoned properties laws beginning in 1915. The single trustee system were compounded in the 1930s by new
travel regulation and passport laws blocking the return of
Armenians to Turkey to reclaim their property.[38] Several
other archives in Turkey are either closed to the public or
require special permission to conduct research: the archives of the Armenian patriarchate in Istanbul; the archives
of the Directorate General of Foundations (*Vakıflar Genel
Müdürlüğü*); the archives of the State Treasury (*Milli Em-
lak ya da Hazine*). These last two include the archives
of the Directorate General of Land Registry and Cadas-
trate (*Tapu ve Kadastro Genel Müdürlüğü*), which, like the
confiscated immovable assets that are their subject, were
transferred after the genocide to the Directorate General
of Foundations and the Treasury.[39] Archival abyss and

---

37 Suciyan, *The Armenians in Modern Turkey*, p. 1.
38 Compare Ekmekçioğlu, *Recovering Armenia*; Suciyan, *The Armenians
    in Modern Turkey*; Üngör, *The Making of Modern Turkey*; Üngör and
    Polatel, *Confiscation and Destruction*.
39 Compare *2012 Beyannamesi: İstanbul Ermeni Vakıflarının El Konan
    Mülkleri / 2012 Declaration: The Seized Properties of Armenian
    Foundations in Istanbul*, ed. by Mehmet Atılgan and others (Istanbul:
    Hrant Dink Vakfı Yayınları, 2012) <https://hrantdink.org/tr/bolis/

blockage of access to these archives reproduce the confiscation and destruction of liquid assets, sacred sites, and immovable property, including homes, shops, farms, gardens, orchards, mills, and both cultivated and uncultivated plots of land, as well as movable livestock[40] borne of the Ottoman elite zeal for Turkification and Muslimization in the eastern parts of the empire, including in Diyarbakır.[41]

Working in official archives is akin to facing 'an active act of production that prepares facts for historical intelligibility'.[42] Armenian individuals, communities, and milieux were purged from the official archives and reduced to a cipher. In such a context, the task of the researcher is to develop a method for locating and deciphering omissions that 'silence the past' and deductive strategies for extrapolating that which remains 'unthinkable'.[43] Similarly, Armenian historians and critics remind us how conducting research in these archives and in the secondary sources that reproduce them is like being in an enclosed and darkened chamber with only a small and damaged aperture through which to project Armenian nativity to the land in

---

faaliyetler/projeler/kulturel-miras/149-2012-beyannamesi-istanbul-ermeni-vakiflarinin-el-konan-mulkleri> [accessed 12 November 2022].

40 Kouymjian, 'Confiscation and Destruction: A Manifestation of the Genocidal Process', *Armenian Forum*, 1.3 (1998), pp. 1–12 (pp. 3–4).

41 Dündar, *İttihat Ve Terakki'nin Müslümanları İskan Politikasi (1913–1918)*; Dündar, *Modern Türkiye'nin Şifresi*; *Armenian Tigranakert/Diarbekir and Edessa/Urfa*; Hilmar Kaiser, 'Armenian Property, Ottoman Law and Nationality Policies', in *The First World War as Remembered in the Countries of the Eastern Mediterranean*, ed. by Olaf Farschid, Manfred Kropp, and Stephan Dähne, Beiruter Texte und Studien, 99 (Würzburg: Ergon-Verlag, 2006), pp. 49–71 (pp. 66 and 70) <https://nbn-resolving.org/urn:nbn:de:gbv:3:5-91478>; Kévorkian, *Le Génocide des Arméniens*; Üngör, *The Making of Modern Turkey*; Üngör and Polatel, *Confiscation and Destruction*.

42 Michel-Rolph Trouillot, *Silencing the Past: Power and the Production of History* (Boston, MA: Beacon Press, 1995), p. 48.

43 Trouillot, *Silencing the Past*, p. 70.

distorted fragments. We learn how these distortions com-
pel the researcher to feel and to imagine that which has
been erased.[44]

Armenian literary critic and philosopher Marc Nichanian, for instance, has reflected the impossibility of reconstructing a factual history of the extermination of Ottoman
Armenians in the late nineteenth and early twentieth centuries under such conditions of historical unthinkability.[45]
He argues that pushing back against the archive's non-
existence, its blanks and silences, dampens the researcher's
historical acuity and at the same time fixates the researcher
traumatically, forcing the researcher to enter a traumatic
field of enclosure only to face a painful discordance between working through history and offering up a politics
of mourning. In moving otherwise from this apparatus of
enclosure built by 'genocidal will',[46] Nichanian distances
himself from factual modes of representation and documentation that reproduce the archival bias of erasure only
to replace it with finitude. The violence and monstrosity of the genocidal will and its ever-present and ongoing
attack on memory cannot be captured by documentary
practices that imply graspability and compensation, argues
Nichanian. Instead, he proposes to refashion testimony as
monument[47] as an excruciating yet creative activity around
the impossibility of mourning rather than a finite factual
achievement that demands the transparent understanding
of mass violence. Nichanian is on the lookout for interpret-

---

44   See Ahıska, 'Occidentalism and Registers of Truth'; Ekmekçioğlu, *Re-
     covering Armenia*; Navaro, 'The Aftermath of Mass Violence'; Nich-
     anian, *Writers of Disaster*; Nichanian, *The Historiographic Perversion*;
     Suciyan, *The Armenians in Modern Turkey*.
45   Nichanian, *Writers of Disaster*, p. 3.
46   Nichanian, *The Historiographic Perversion*, p. 9.
47   Ibid., p. 94.

ative and imaginative narrative strategies and methodologies to see through the authoritarian archival erasure that locks the researcher into methodological dead-ends.

Powerfully circumventing archival dead-ends of structural denialism in their respective works, both Talin Suciyan and Lerna Ekmekçioğlu have recently rendered Armenian existence legible by turning to Armenian-language newspapers, memoirs, oral narratives, and their personal herstories.[48] Rejecting intellectual absorption in the defeatism generated by factual fundamentalism, Suciyan sets to work demonstrating how genocide denialism is constitutive of the racist structuring of the Turkish state's historical and legal apparatus. While denialism is further fed by the process of 'becoming-diaspora',[49] in so far as the overwhelming majority of surviving Armenians were forced to leave their ancestral lands as a result of legal and social campaigns, for the few who remained in Turkey, Lerna Ekmekçioğlu argues, the intimate spheres of 'domesticated survival',[50] religion and spirituality, and feminist politics became productive arenas in which to retrieve Armenian existence against the archival chokehold.

Rather than digging through the oppressor's archive to find proof and validation, these approaches reject the distorted terms of archival gaslighting's fabricated causality. Taking a cue from Saidiya Hartman's work, these approaches attempt to think through that which has been forced to stay in 'the position of the unthought'.[51]

---

48   Suciyan, *The Armenians in Modern Turkey*; Ekmekçioğlu, *Recovering Armenia*.

49   Suciyan, *The Armenians in Modern Turkey*, pp. 20 and 27.

50   Ibid., p. 122.

51   Saidiya V. Hartman and Frank B. Wilderson III, 'The Position of the Unthought', *Qui Parle*, 13.2 (2003), pp. 183–201 <https://doi.org/10.1215/quiparle.13.2.183>.

Hartman's point is to expose the chokehold supremacist archives represent, limiting as they do the researcher's ability to uncover the unrelenting violence of transatlantic slavery and its brutal wake in the ongoing legacy of enslavement after emancipation in North America. Rendering 'what cannot be known' thinkable is not Hartman's project, for such a move would propose a coherent and hopeful corrective to the archive. The goal is thus not to speak truth to the archive by approximating the lived experience of slavery. Nor is it to civilize the archive by 'giving voice' to the enslaved.[52] Hartman sets herself the task of developing a methodological strategy ('critical fabulation'[53]) whereby the scholar authorizes herself to cautiously speculate about and rearrange the experience of enslavement.

If for Hartman the 'unthought' is the 'narrative re-straint'[54] that makes it impossible to think the relationship between the structural brutality of enslavement and the racist forms of archival and everyday violence that developed after emancipation (the 'afterlife of slavery'), then for Suci-yan and Ekmekçioğlu, the position of the unthought would be the position of the social reproduction of archival denial that the Armenian genocide ever occurred or that Armenians were and are native to the land. In a similar fashion to Hartman, the methodological strategies of shadowing, omission, and eclipsing used by Suciyan and Ekmekçioğlu work to surface the denialist structural constitution of the Turkish regime without abandoning contact with historical experience. While the two historians do not creatively

---

52   Saidiya Hartman, 'Venus in Two Acts', *Small Axe: A Caribbean Journal of Criticism*, 12.2 (2008), pp. 1–14 (p. 12) <https://doi.org/10.1215/-12-2-1>.

53   Ibid., p. 11.

54   Ibid.

fashion stories in Hartman's sense, they do rely on meticu-
lously researched narratives that turbulently *feel in* rather
than *fill in* the archival blanks. As responses to the limits
of the archive, their accounts seek to 'resurrect' the 'impossible story' by amplifying 'the impossibility of its telling'.[55]
Faced with the limits of the archive, inspired by
Suciyan and Ekmekçioğlu's methodological handsprings
through the obstacle course of legibility, and seeking
to centre genocide's 'evidentiary ecologies'[56] via eco-
redaction, a form of Hartman's 'critical fabulation',[57]
I wonder if ecological elements that make up the
landscape of the long-ruined Dikranagerd can better be
understood as resurgent fragments of a crime scene that
live suspended in time and held hostage under 'house
arrest' by the denialist Turkish state.

MULBERRY AFFECTS

I ask an Armenian writer from Dikranagerd questions
about mulberry trees. A few months into our correspond-
ence, Varduhi recounts her research with relatives and
acquaintances on her roots near the Tigris riverbank. She
tells me that beneath the foundations of Dicle University,
directly across from Hewsel Gardens and just below her
grandparents' Armenian and Syriac village of Qerebash,
lies the rubble of another Armenian and Syriac village.
Qeterbel was famous for its clean water, watermelons, and

---

55 Ibid.
56 Kristina Lyons, 'Decomposition as Life Politics: Soils, *Selva*, and Small
    Farmers under the Gun of the US-Colombian War on Drugs', *Cultural
    Anthropology*, 31.1 (2016), pp. 56–81 <https://doi.org/10.14506/
    ca31.1.04>.
57 Hartman, 'Venus in Two Acts', p. 11.

orchards.[58] Varduhi tells me that rubble from the buildings and monuments destroyed by the Turkish military
in 2015 during the Siege of Sur — the ancient Christian
neighbourhood in which she grew up — as well as the
centenarian trees that were erased, were all deposited into
an area near the Gardens atop the rubble of the old village. I look up the two villages in a book titled *Amed*, the
Kurdish name for Diyarbakır, published by the Diyarbakır
Municipality.[59] The municipality is known for its efforts to
open up space for memorialization practices that counter
the Turkish Republic's official historiography and its denial of the Armenian genocide. I see that Qeterbel is not
mentioned. Qerebash, on the other hand, is depicted as a
Kurmanji-speaking Kurdish village that was the target of
assimilation policies enacted by the Turkish government
in 1934 with the aim of settling Turkish migrants from
Bulgaria into the area. The two Armenian/Syriac villages
have vanished from the book.

When I began searching for traces of mulberry trees
and of the village of Qeterbel in accounts that challenge
this vanishing effect, I had to un-learn in order to relearn, search through fragmented layers of time and space.
In the near complete absence of local Armenian or Syriac testimonies about the anti-Christian pogroms of 1895,
Joost Jongerden and Jelle Verheij read the reports of foreign missionaries, the Ottoman archives, and the conson-
ant secondary sources and Turkish nationalist memoirs
against the grain in an attempt to reconstruct the void

---

58 Qeterbel, now in the site of the Dicle University campus, is spelled
in various sources also as Kıtırbıl, Kiterbèl, Gheterpel, Qatrabel, and
Keterbel. *Social Relations in Ottoman Diyarbekir*, ed. by Jongerden and
Verheij, p. 307.

59 Amed Tîgrîs and Yıldız Çakar, *Amed: Coğrafya, Tarih, Kültür* (Diyarbakır: Diyarbakır Büyükşehir Belediyesi Yayınları, 2015).

that mass violence against non-Muslim, non-Turks opened
in Ottoman Diyarbekir's demographic and socioeconomic
life.[60] In their respective accounts, the village of Qeterbel
emerges in 1895 as the site of pogroms against Armenians
and Syriacs in which their properties were confiscated and
transferred to Muslim collaborators of the Committee of
Union and Progress regime, which had ordered the pil-
laging and burning of the village.[61] The village was the site
of a massacre carried out by Muslim militia in which about
five hundred Christians were murdered.[62] Ümit Üngör and
Mehmet Polatel further confirm that the villages of Qeterbel and Qerebash became targets in a new wave of mass
arrests and violence around the time of the 1915 genocide.[63] The silk and *pushi* headscarf industries operated
primarily by Armenians and Syriacs became extinct after
the 1915 annihilation of the Diyarbakırite Christians, with
their assets, including mulberry orchards sold at auction
to Muslim settlers who began re-settling from the Cauca-
sus and the Balkans, due to state policy.[64] Not only were
these refugee-settlers resettled there soon after the genocide; they were also given the annihilated Christians' seeds,
animals, ploughs, vineyards, orchards, and gardens.[65] During the 1920s, the ruined village of Qeterbel became a
model site of Republican developmentalist zeal as the government sought to revitalize '5,000 acres of barren land'
by sending in experts ranging from veterinarians to health

---

60   *Social Relations in Ottoman Diyarbekir*, ed. by Jongerden and Verheij.

61   Ibid., pp. 73–74, p. 334.

62   Jelle Verheij, 'Diyarbekir and the Armenian Crisis of 1895', in *Social Relations in Ottoman Diyarbekir*, ed. by Jongerden and Verheij, pp. 85–147 (p. 105).

63   Üngör and Polatel, *Confiscation and Destruction*, p. 68.

64   Ibid., p. 44.

65   Üngör, *The Making of Modern Turkey*, p. 146.

inspectors to examine and monitor the land and its inhabitants, building a ranch with technical equipment from
Europe, and distributing free saplings, chicken, and seeds
as well as pesticides. The erasure of the village from the
toponymical map was completed in the 1930s when its
name became Turkified as 'Eğlence', meaning 'fun' in Turkish.[66]

Another attempt to document former Armenian ownership of village land here and plots at Hewsel Gardens was
to conduct archival research on local journals published in
Armenian in and around Dikranagerd/Diyarbakır with the
assistance of a research collaborator, Muraz Sarangil. The
journal Դգլիս (Tigris) was published in Dikranagerd
on various dates at least as from the late Ottoman period
and at various intervals. The nine issues of the Դգլիս-
Tigris that we were able to access also contained articles
addressing resettlement. They too included missing per-
sons' reports from Diyarbakırite families who had lost their
relatives and loved ones in 1915 and were still trying to find
news of them through the magazine. Although rare, these
magazines contained letters from compatriots, poems, and
phone numbers and messages for events, including picnics
and late-night dinners organized by the association's headquarters and branches. After the genocide, Դգլիս-Tigris
resurfaced in New York as a weekly magazine under the
title of Nor Dikranagerd (New Diyarbakır). The association
that published the New York magazine, the Dikranagerd
Compatriotic and Reconstruction Union, was a solidarity
organization that held large-scale meetings in the halls of
the Ramgavar Party, an Armenian diaspora party that maintained relations with Soviet Armenia. An important goal of
the association was the establishment of the satellite city

---

66   Ibid., p. 244.

district of Nor Dikranagerd, to be built on land located between the satellite cities of Nor Malatya (New Malatya) and Nor Sepasdya (New Sivas) in the Armenian Soviet Socialist Republic capital of Yerevan.

In the twelve issues of *Nor Dikranagerd* we accessed, reports on financial and infrastructural matters regarding the construction of the New Dikranagerd neighbourhood in Yerevan were supplemented with essays on the Armenian names for sites of historical import located along the shores of the Tigris, such as Karsun Mangants for Kırklar Mountain and Barda Buren for the Erdebil Mansion, along with a history of Ten Eyes Bridge recounting a journey by boat from the bridge to Mosul, Baghdad.[67] Reporting on massacres was a significant theme in the journal's pages. Among the letters received by the journal, Tovmas Mıgırdiçyan is noteworthy in that he presents his research on Diyarbakır in application to the association for its publication as a book. His letter includes photos of the village of Qerebash. Mıgırdiçyan maintains that he has carried out research on Diyarbakır and has fifteen to twenty articles ready for publication, several of which contain 'political secrets' about which he swore in April 1921 to the British Foreign Office not to publish or make public for ten years.[68] Now that the deadline had passed, the author was seeking assistance from the journal's New York editors to publish it in their pages. An open letter from 1938 to the association's headquarters and branches by the Armenian patriarch of Turkey, Mesrop Naroyan, mentions the existence of Armenians still living in Diyarbakır and recounts how the church was damaged in a fire on the night of 24 April 1938, the eighteenth anniversary of the genocide. The patriarch also

---

67   Yeğişe Çerçiyan, *Nor Dikaranagerd*, 20.2 (1937), pp. 5–6.
68   Tovmas Mıgırdiçyan, 'Letter', *Nor Dikaranagerd,* 20.3 (1938), pp. 9–11.

notes that the church expected to receive financial support from the Armenian residents of Diyarbakır.[69] An excerpt from a letter from Tovmas Zavzavatcıyan illustrates how, during the anti-Armenian pogrom of 1895, the massacres lasted for three days, with the Diyarbakır Armenian church of St. Sarkis destroyed just after the plunder of the Qeterbel Syriac church and the killing of the entire village, along with its priest, Kas Ablahat.[70]

The *Tigris-Dikris Almanac* published in 1946 provides more room for imagination in reconstructing the landscape of the Tigris riverbank. The almanac was prepared by the Aleppo branch of the Dikranagerd Compatriotic and Reconstruction Union. Although headquartered in New York, the solidarity association had by the mid-forties some thirty active branches, located primarily in Aleppo and Beirut. Armenian villages along the shores of Tigris and near the Hewsel Gardens were portrayed as recreational places of ecological abundance where Armenian peasants cultivated the land. In an article compiled by A. Kuyum-cuyan in the *Tigris-Dikris Almanac*, we learn that silk farming was completely in the hands of Armenians, with the writer listing the names of Armenian family businesses.[71] In Hewsel Gardens, there was a tradition for people to invite each other to drink tea at the *manafşalık* (violet gardens) during the Christian festival of carnival (Lent). With the arrival of spring, first the almond groves would be frequented in Hewsel, then the rose gardens (*güllük*), and especially the Ğam garden (*gam götürmez*). These are gardens cultivated today by Kurdish farmers without any sign of previous Armenian cultivation.

69   Mesrop Naroyan, 'Open Letter', *Nor Dikaranagerd*, 21.2 (1938), pp. 9–10.
70   Zavzavatcıyan B. Tovmas, 'Letter', *Nor Dikaranagerd*, 21 (1939), p. 5.
71   A. Kuyumcuyan, entry in *Tigris-Dikris Almanac* (Aleppo: Digranakerd Compatriotic and Reconstruction Union, 1946), p. 97.

Qeterbel emerges in these essays as the site of old vineyards with endemic grapes, watermelons, and mulberries.
The Qeterbel vineyards were frequented by groups of
people spending the summer in tents by the shore.[72] *Ami-
dayi Artsakanqner* (Echoes of Amida), published by the
New York-based Armenian American writer Dikran Mgunt
in 1950,[73] gives further insights into the ecological features
of the area between the city and the Tigris riverbank including Ali Pınar and Qeterbel. The village of Ali Punar (Ali
Pınar) was a recreational destination site for well-off citizens who visited during the summer, on Sundays, and after
church to picnic among the vineyards, gardens, and under
the almond trees. The villagers were very poor and resigned
to their fate because most of the barley and chickpea were
planted on fields that belonged to the village chief (village lord, ethnicity unspecified) and most of the income
went to him while taxes paid to the state were taken from
the small amount of produce left in the peasants' hands.
Qeterbel appears in this account as a Syriac Christian village, of fifty households. In 1893, the Tigris overflowed and
changed its course, eradicating a large forest, the account
notes. According to the narrator, because of this once-in-
a-hundred-years event, the Tigris River came right up to
the entrance of Qeterbel village establishing proximity between the village and city centre via the river. Two years
later, during the three-day pogrom of 1895, Mgunt reports,
villagers sought refuge in the church. When the church was
set on fire, they emerged fighting. The majority of the men
were slaughtered, and the women and children were dis-

---

72   Քաղբրցի, entry in *Tigris-Dikris Almanac* (Aleppo: Digranakerd Com-
      patriotic and Reconstruction Union, 1946), p. 32.

73   Dikran Mgunt, ԱՄԻՏԱՅԻ ԱՐՁԱԳԱՆԳՆԵՐ [Echoes of Amida]
      (Weehawken, NJ: Dikran Spear, 1950; repr. Antelias, Lebanon: Cilicia
      Bookstore, 2019).

tributed to Muslim homes.[74] The book debunks the myth
of peaceful coexistence between the Armenian and Kurdish communities by providing insights into everyday life
laced with extreme caution and attention on the part of the
Armenians and Syriacs seeking to avoid potential conflict.

Visiting the approximate site of Qeterbel was another
attempt to come closer to an understanding of the an-
archic fragments left by the genocidal spiral on the landscape. On my first visit to the destroyed village in 2019, I
arrive at an untended and untamed landscape dotted with
feral centenarian mulberry trees. My guide, a Kurdish professor specializing in endemic species and native seeds who
runs an ecological project by the Tigris River together with
a few academics-turned-farmers who were summarily dis-
missed from their university jobs in the Turkish academic
purge of 2016, is reluctant to take me to the site, as he
thinks 'there's nothing there'. Although the site now be-
longs to Dicle University, it has long been 'abandoned', he
notes. In a moment of profound self-reflection, my friend
Hasan, whose Armenian family had to convert to Islam
for self-protection, shortly after the genocide, wants to see
the site even if 'there is nothing there'. Hasan is interested
in retracing his genealogical roots, uncovering the circumstances surrounding his family's conversion. The research,
he says, has piqued his desire to reconstruct his personal
history. We wander for a long time through feral plots in a
fragile attempt akin to premonition that it is there — somewhere, around the corner, after the next turnout, behind
the next hill, perhaps. After becoming disoriented several
times in this area due to the absence of site-specific directions, and with the assistance of a map drawn for me
and Hasan by an elderly Kurdish interlocutor, some digital

---

74   Ibid., p. 235.

maps, and directions we request from passers-by along the way, we finally arrive at a feral spot overlooking the riverbank and the distant face of the ancient city wall of Diyarbakır.

The professor, now visibly excited, studies the abandoned feral landscape and is impressed by the sight of indigenous centenarian mulberry trees. He goes on feeding us information. 'In fact', he begins to recount, 'these trees take about five to ten years to begin bearing fruit… The mulberry fruit is a collection of many tiny fruits joined together, itself the result of a process of inflorescence… These trees prefer drained soil, but they are tolerant of drought and frost, too… They make great shade, which is essential for the summer heat…' The site that had first appeared featureless to the professor later becomes intriguing enough for its ecological habitats to inspire him to share essential biological facts. While listening to him, I notice the stone wall ruins of an old, derelict building, a few centenarian mulberry trees scattered throughout the grass, and a vast array of younger, feral mulberry trees — all an indication of the orchards that once covered the area around the village. Perhaps the indigenous seeds native to Kurdistan that the professor is so adamant about collecting with his farmer friends were of Armenian provenance after all.

The stone foundations peek out from among the stand of mulberries of Varduhi's grandparents' now-ruined village. Whether they strictly evidence past Armenian and Syriac habitation or not, these centenarians materialize ecological roots amid ongoing sieges. Hasan is silent. He says he feels overwhelmed by the site. The centenarians seem to work their way in and through him, like affective matter. Having long understood himself as a Kurdish man with strong sympathies for the Kurdish movement, he opens to the possibility of identifying as an Armenian man from this land and reclaiming his complex nativity to it in new light. I feel an uneasy silence weigh heavy on my shoulders as the sight of the centenarians prompts me to consider the possibility that we have perhaps trespassed on an unrecognized massacre site. Mulberries urge me to unsettle my own academic and political complicity in not noticing, thus perpetuating a distinction between abandoned and annihilated ecological sites, an epistemically violent distinction that permits the tacit maintenance of denialist conceits and schemes. We set off to leave.

On our way back, I reconsider Marc Nichanian's observation that in a realm of denialism, facts are doomed to be inoperative, and documentation is an inadequate intellectual and political disposition.[75] I take refuge in these reflections to consider these centenarian mulberry trees and their feral companions to be 'testimonies as monument'.[76] They 'escape'[77] the gaze of the official archive as resistant roots that continue to feed on more than a hundred years of destruction and solitude. Held hostage under a suspended curse but still readying themselves for an archive that is still 'to come in the anterior future',[78] the trees challenge the logocentric scaffolding of Turkish archives that erase or reduce ecological massacre sites to background effect.

Mulberry affects.

---

75   Nichanian, *The Historiographic Perversion*.
76   Ibid., p. 83.
77   Ibid., p. 103.
78   Ibid., p. 114.

ECO-REDACTION: AN AN-ARCHIC COUNTER TO DENIALISM

Char 1: Stumps

'Char' — charred material, the stuff of charcoal — is an idiom of blacked-out redaction. Char invites me to think with ecological edges-in-the-making that exist under archival and on-the-ground erasure of interspecies life by the sovereign Turkish rule and that persist in the ongoing wake of genocidal spiral in the era of climate change. Char regis-

Figure 1. Char 1: Stumps, photo by author, 2019.

ters that disasters have already arrived, have been ongoing, and have been responded to. Char asks us to pay attention to those durable colonial enclosures, genocidal aftermaths, military sieges, and capitalist wreckage that are impossible to metabolize.

The first image is of charred stumps from a centennial mulberry tree on the outskirts of the Hewsel Gardens felled by chemical weaponry during the siege of 2015. I blackened the already charred stumps further to amplify their alleged status as non-life according to the genocidal optic of the state and to point to their invisibilization (and hence their uncomplication) as ecological rubble that rots in the background.

Char 2: The Wall

Occupation is as much about construction as it is about destruction. The wall in figure 2 was erected soon after the blockade of 2015 to prevent Kurdish youths from escaping to the Gardens and attacking the military convoys in self-defence. The livelihood of Kurdish farmers, based as it was on cultivating the Hewsel Gardens, was completely cut off during the siege.

I blackened the grey concrete wall to amplify its occupying power.

Figure 2. Char 2: The Wall, photo by author, 2019.

Figure 3. Char 3: Mulberry Affects, photo by author, 2019.

Char 3: Mulberry Affects

'To live in the habitus of denial is akin to perpetually setting the cycle of death alight', writes Aylin Vartanyan Dilaver.[79] 'Imagine a tree that feeds on the tar of fear, flowing from its roots to its trunk and to the fire of anger. The tar feeds the fire. The fire makes the trunk glow. In time, the tree sprouts leaves of fire and bears fruits of tar. This poison from the roots keeps the tree erect, but it does not keep the tree alive.'[80]

Just before the genocide, I relearn, mulberry trees grew both inside and outside Diyarbakır's city centre: in the back yards of urban houses and in the Hewsel Gardens.[81] As with the living-dead tree that Vartanyan Dilaver imagines, emblematic of an unfinished mourning, the mulberry's layered meanings prompt the imagination to recast the contested and violently traversed claims of nativity to the land and the right to repatriation. The tree conveys the sense of something ongoing, collective, intimate, and ecological about the impacts that episodes of mass violence leave on multispecies worlds in the denialist longue durée.

On my first visit to what I think might be Qeterbel, I arrive at an erased landscape dotted with feral centenarian mulberry trees. I have blackened the trees in figure 3 to amplify the sense of ongoing ecocide present in more-than-human traces.

---

79 Vartanyan Dilaver, 'From Longing to Belong to Shaping the Longing' (unpublished doctoral thesis in progress), no page number.

80 Ibid., translation mine.

81 Ahmet Taşğin and Marcello Mollica, 'Disappearing Old Christian Professions in the Middle East: The Case of Diyarbakır Pushee-Makers', *Middle Eastern Studies*, 51.6 (2 November 2015), pp. 922–31 <https://doi.org/10.1080/00263206.2015.1044525>.

Figure 4. Char 4: Seed, photo by author, 2019.

Char 4: Seed

Before the Siege of 2015–16 commenced, hundreds of eco-projects were realized with non-hybrid seeds and pesticide-free farming by eco-activists and Yazidi refugee women who in 2014 fled the Yazidi Genocide in their ancestral homeland of Sinjar in Iraqi Kurdistan and settled in the refugee camp of Diyarbakır. Since the occupation of Sur and its surrounding areas, they are all largely ruined. All signs of previous communal work and cultivation have been erased. Nothing remotely resembling a site of cultivation appears before the passer-by. Plants have been uprooted and are gone for good. Plots have become subdivisions of a wasteland.

Azad cultivates a plot of land across from Hewsel near the Tigris River with a group of academics expelled during the purge of 2016 in Turkey and refugee families. Together, they work to create an indigenous seed bank of pest-resistant plants. Azad stresses the difficulties of putting decolonial ecological principles into practice under the state's sporadic spiral of military sieges where 'war is the climate', as people put it.

I blacked out some of the seeds stored in the ecologically constructed home that houses the seed bank to amplify the ongoing ecocide.

Figure 5. Lungs, photo courtesy of the Schwules Museum,
Berlin, 2018.

Zine: 'Lungs' (figures 5 and 6)

The zine is a medium of lexical eco-redaction. Titled *Lungs*,
the fanzine/object is a simple lexical inventory of Hewsel
Gardens. Words related to or associated with the Gardens'
biodiversity are listed in succession, forming a catalogue
of raw data arranged in cross-referenced thematic lists that
codify those things that have penetrated the Gardens. The
lists include such things as endemic plant and animal species, aquatic resources, fountains, orchards' names, Armenian, Syriac, and Kurdish musical instruments once played
in the recreational areas of the Gardens, news reports about
blockades, phrases from the UNESCO protocol, construction machinery and materials, the brand names of chemical
pesticides, and guns. I produced one hundred copies, some

Figure 6. Lungs, photo courtesy of the Schwules Museum,
Berlin, 2018.

of which were placed in bookshops in Dikranagerd/Amed
after obtaining the consent of shop owners. Others were
exhibited in December 2017 as part of a collective show
titled *Koloni* at Abud Efendi Konağı, Istanbul, and again in
March 2018 at the Schwules Museum in Berlin.

ACKNOWLEDGEMENTS

I wish to thank various people for their contribution to
this research; the ICI Berlin cohort (2018–20), for pre-
paring me to hear multispecies heartbeats through epistemological an-archy and for stimulating debates on racism
and archival omissions through the work of Fred Moten,
Saidiya Hartman, and Christina Sharpe; Muraz Sarangil
for his archival work, directions, and fellowship; Emre Can

Dağlıoğlu, Rober Koptaş, Silva Özyerli, Talin Suciyan, and Vahé Tachjian for their archival suggestions; Kevser Güler, Derya Bayraktaroğlu, and Aylime Aslı Demir for their curatorial perspective on utopia, as well as their gracious invitation that allowed me to experience the recalcitrant and queer world of *colony* in Istanbul and Berlin; and Handan Coşkun and Remzi Yıldırım for their rooting friendship and research collaboration. Einstein Stiftung Berlin fieldwork grant was instrumental to the completion of this article. The usual disclaimers apply.

Who's Afraid of Ideology?

MARWA ARSANIOS

LAND MAKING. LANDING IN THE RESEARCH SITE

The status of ownership always entails a voiding of the owned other. A temporal and spatial emptying out that enables the act of possession. If one thinks of land as the object of ownership, then the first thing that comes to mind is the invisible creatures that live in the soil and underground, such as bacteria. My artistic practice conceptualizes the void as a moving and murmuring entity: even if one needs a microscope to see it and an affective predisposition to feel it, it exists as such. My work questions the very idea of void as a passive entity. Void becomes a haunting matter, made of human and more-than-human elements, that transports us to a communal world that exists at the edges of capitalist structures of property, ownership, and legality. If voiding is a multilayered process through which colonial and capitalist violence crushed Indigenous lives by fabricating registers of ownership and legality, it also bears the affective echoes and ecological markers of such destruction.

Working with a few communes that were built on reappropriated land, I ask: How can one think of ecological
markers, traces of voiding, and communalizing of the land?
What kind of methodology would capture not only the
ruination of land and displacement of humans, but also
the world-making and resistance of communities that are
involved in processes of reappropriation? How to perceive
such voiding? With a focus on ecologies of displacement
and resistance, I listen to murmuring landscapes made
of humans, plants, rocks, fertilizers, preserved vegetables.
This is to see what happens when life heals and regenerates
in communal terms amidst war in militarized geographies
while bearing traces of long-term violence.

The text moves through different geographies between
northern Syria (Rojava) and Iraqi Kurdistan, where I encountered women who are shaping new relationships to
their lands and rearticulating their communal lives. These
relatively small, slow, and supposedly low-key endeavours
yield great insights, showing how new ecological paradigms and politics are being born out of the necessity to
survive in situations of war. They can potentially create a
paradigmatic shift in power relations.

THE SICK FIG TREE. THE PLAIN. THE SUN.

While touring a cooperative in the region of Serekanieh,
in northern Syria, we listen to the agricultural engineer
describe what they are trying to build on this land recently
appropriated by the autonomous region of Rojava after the
regime was pushed back in 2011. The land appears dry
but there are many wells on the plot. The conversation
below captures how reappropriation, work, maintenance,
and care for a land can heal years of industrial usage and
how the double voiding of the state's grip on the land

Figure 1. Wild plant. Author's photo.

and then its retrieval has created the potential for another kind of relationship and reorganization of the plot. It is now a cooperative run by agricultural workers who were previously employed by the state and paid a daily wage. Historically, the Kurdish population from this region was systematically impoverished and had little access to land ownership.

Fragments from a conversation:

— This land was managed by the Syrian Libyan company before it went bankrupt

During the war the villagers around cut all the trees because they needed wood to heat themselves

Let's go see how they are irrigating the trees there

We have planted three thousand trees

We don't have enough means, there is a water scarcity, at the moment there is a water tank there and it's irrigating each individual plant, we are trying to keep it green

Here they are irrigating as well

— I am afraid of snakes

— Look at the sheep

This is the hospital for the sheep

There are the raisins, the apricots, the mango trees

There is more until the end of the field

We planted all this only five months ago

— Mango needs a lot of water

— This is the fig and there are the pomegranate

These bigger fig trees are from the regime's time but the smaller ones here are all ours

This the regime's fig

— It looks ill

— People say that during the regime's time there was fig and pomegranate here

— Let's take a picture of the regime's fig tree

These are our fig trees here they are in better shape

— What is this?

— It's wild herbs

This is called sower milk

It's very good for toothache

The small figs are ours

The produce is not the most important, our aim is for the tree to grow and for the field to become green

Here are the apples

— How can apple grow here?

It's very warm

— People used to say this area is not useful for trees

But it's not true, this was just the regime's politics

The politics of impoverishment

They just wanted to grow wheat here and take it for themselves, like a colonial extractionist force

The other side of the border in Bakur, in Turkey, it is so green. The agricultural state politics were better on the other side

If the people of Bakur had the Rojava land in their hands it would have been an amazing place (laughs)

There are the raisins, we can go see them

This is wild zaatar

Some of the raisins are dying, you can see that, but it's difficult with the water scarcity

Anyway, come back in two years, this will be a paradise on earth

Let's go back

— Are you afraid that the regime will put their hands on this land again?

— Even if there won't be a deal with the regime, the important thing is that this land will become green

— Do you use fertilizers?

— Yes in some cases we have to, but they are not chemical

This land is very fertile

Figure 2. Alternative medicine. Author's photo.

WILD HERBS. FERTILITY. FERTILIZERS

Khalisseh practices as an alternative medicine doctor in the Kurdish town of Derbesiyeh in northern Syria. She talks about many cases that she has healed, a few of them being fertility problems.

> It's a practice I have learned from my grandmother, I was assisting her
>
> Since I was ten I had the curiosity to follow my grandmother in her work
>
> I started doing some experiments for medicine, I would try it on myself before anyone else
>
> Since 1995 I have been practicing in my house, since five months I opened the clinic here

I had the opportunity to work in a hospital but I refused

I worked as a nurse and I also worked in a lab

I first diagnose the patients, if I have doubts I send them to do the analysis or to do an echography, then they come back to me with the analysis

I am an alternative medicine doctor, it's also called herbal medicine

I don't sell medicine, patients often ask me for herbs, but I don't give them away like this, herbs can be very strong on the body

For example I am often asked for this herb called Oshrok, I ask them what do you need it for? They say to lose weight. Of course I refuse to give it to them because Oshrok is not for weight loss it is for very strong cases of constipation

It is like a tranquilizer, it is very strong

After diagnosis I make a special medicine for each case

I treated fifty-six cases of depression this year, I usually massage the belly button and the lower back. I try to adjust the belly button and re-centre it

The most common diseases are spine, joints, back and neck problems, I treat all of those

Sometimes it can take two weeks to heal and sometimes months

I diagnosed a lot of cancers as well

In the spring I go to the fields myself to get the herbs

I have treated a lot of cases of eczema

For example for the spine, I have a special mix, olive oil, honey wax, snake oil, barakeh seed

You will heal

This is my special mix

After 2011 there was a lot of difficulties receiving all our herbs and material

Most of the resources were coming from Damascus before

After the war, roads were closed it was very difficult to get the basic products

In the spring I get a lot of the herbs as well, chamomile, the khetmiyeh, wild rihan, wild zaatar, I go to the mountains and get them. Zayzafoun, malisseh, all this I get it from here. The barakeh seed, the helbeh, the yansoun, sesame for the oil. All of that I get from here

I go to the wilderness and discover new herbs, and try them on myself, if they don't have a bad effect it means they might have some benefits

For example there is a lot of herbs that are detoxifiers. For example camomille is detoxifying

For example wild zaatar is a tranquilizer, for the colon, for the flu it cleans the lungs, for the liver, it detoxifies, for the removal of fat, for high tension

The wild rihan has the same benefits

The jaadeh is very strong and it can ruin the liver, so one should not abuse it; it is good for the high sugar, by washing the feet with it

The helbeh, is good for pancreas the heart, it can be boiled, it eliminates inflammation

It is good if men ha[ve] weak sperm

Koronfol is a very strong tranquilizer

And it is also used for people who have fertility problems.

The radish seed, is very good for erection problems

Coconut oil for increasing the hair

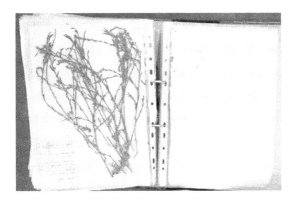

Figure 3. A diary. Author's photo.

If a baby is cramping you can put the naranj oil

She used to do mixes with this herb called jwayfeh, this herb doesn't exist anymore, or we can't find it

I have also treated people with war scares. Because of operations sometimes they lose the sensitivity on the scar

Also burns, if they are at the beginning

WILD PLANTS. FOOD. NGOS.

In a cooperative in Hermel, east of the Bekaa Valley in Lebanon, on the border with Syria, Khadija is running a workshop teaching Syrian women living in neighbouring refugee camps how to preserve seasonal vegetables for the winter. All these women who come from rural areas carry so much agricultural knowledge. They have been made landless by the Syrian regime, and struggle to survive without a plot that they can cultivate. Their relationship to this new place is built through their agricultural and food knowledge.

Khadija is cooking green fava beans on one side of the oven and tomato paste on the other. While explaining every step in the cooking process and the benefits of each vegetable — its type, origin, and local source — she pours the beans and the paste into a jar, closes it, and turns it upside down on the table. 'That's how you keep the pressure in and avoid any air leaks.' Each jar will serve as a meal for the family, with a portion of rice on the side. It's spring, and the contents of these jars will be eaten next fall or winter. Buying fava in March is very cheap, since it's in season. 'We are learning how to eat cheap and healthy', she says while stirring the tomato paste, which has been cooking on a low fire for the past thirty minutes. 'Always buy seasonal vegetables and conserve them for the coming season. Each season has its vegetables and each vegetable has its preservation process.'

I met Khadija in her cooperative, which consists of a three-room workshop and a big kitchen. It is surrounded by a plot of land that she inherited from her mother and turned into a food production cooperative, where she grows most of the crops and where women can gather, share knowledge, and learn from each other about food preservation, crop cultivation, seed preservation, and different ways of treating the soil. She has been running this cooperative for seven years, despite the local politics and the tensions with Hezbollah (the dominant party in the area), which often tries to make it difficult for her to continue with the cooperative. Meanwhile, she has continued to pursue her activities, producing seasonal jams and other food provisions that she sells to sustain the cooperative. Regarding the political tensions, she says to me: 'Hezbollah could benefit from the fact that I am creating a micro-economy and transmit forgotten knowledge, but instead all they think about is how to have sole hegemonic power.

They don't want any growth that is outside of their control.' In fact, small independent organizations and cooperatives supported by international funders are usually left to do their work, unless it is believed that they oppose the dominant political power; the latter situation leads to clashes, tensions, and difficulties, such as indirectly pressuring the farmers to slow down their work or to stop it completely.

This cooperative is funded by the United States Agency for International Development (USAID) and has collaborated with different groups since 2013, especially humanitarian refugee organizations. When Khadija was approached by USAID (as part of its program to fight hunger), she was already known for her skills and knowledge regarding the edible and medicinal wild plants she gathers. It is an old practice that many women carry on. Usually it is transmitted to them by their mothers or another elderly woman in the family.

Khadija opens a folder where she has gathered an extensive archive of dried wild edible weeds. She has a precise knowledge of the use and medical benefits of each plant. 'This is precious knowledge from my mother. She was also a farmer and owned this piece of land that I inherited from her.' After each workshop on cheap, healthy food and edible wild plants, the products are equally divided among the women to feed their families.

Since 2012, the flow of refugees from Syria has led about fifty international NGOs to set up camp in the Bekaa region. As the immediate crisis-solving apparatus, they settled in the area with the highest density of refugees. The few food cooperatives and NGOs run by women in the region became spaces where the transmission of knowledge happens. A few have begun to be used as support spaces for refugee women, in collaboration with humanitarian NGOs.

Before 2011 and the eruption of the Syrian revolution, these kind of initiatives (mostly funded by USAID and the EU) had found their place on the map of Lebanon's eco-conscious urban middle class. In urban areas they could sell produce to restaurants and directly to customers at farmer's markets. After 2011, many employed low-wage Syrian women, turning the cooperatives into fully-fledged businesses or transforming themselves into useful spaces for women from the camps — sometimes both.

The cooperative Khadija runs seems to want to re-inforce the politics of the commons through the transmission of a knowledge that is embedded in a very specific geography and seasonal landscape. This knowledge of wild plants, often considered 'bad herbs' in modern agricultural practice, is at the core of this cooperative. What makes this construction of the commons possible in this case is in fact the global aid economy (USAID funding). The cooperative cannot fully sustain itself yet, since the food and herbs it produces don't bring in enough money.

Many non-governmental women's organizations have emerged in the Arab world in the past twenty years, and even more since 2011 to deal with the refugee crisis, a lack of nutritional resources, domestic violence, and women's health issues. Though some do not present themselves as explicitly feminist, many deal with women's issues or create spaces that specifically support women. Others more directly present themselves as feminist through research, discourse, and knowledge production. Often compensating for a lack of state structures, NGO structures work within the global economy and produce discourses that travel within and are shaped by this global economy. While many of these small initiatives adopt a language of 'empowerment', 'development', 'economic independence', and 'women's entrepreneurship', they also function within a

very small locality, and their political struggle often becomes isolated in local politics. Gender essentialism —
'women's empowerment' — overtakes any class or race discourses, which are at the core of internationalist feminist
politics. 'Global womanhood' becomes a category or a class
in itself. Hunger is separated from class and from the failure of states to provide and distribute wealth equally. The
main political aim becomes fighting hunger, without any
reflection on what has caused this hunger — for example,
the failure to subsidize farmers' material needs; the historical mismanagement of water distribution, which has led
to drought in many areas; the overexploitation of underground water (like in the Bekaa Valley); the distribution
or subsidization of fertilizers for farmers, which over many
years has damaged the soil; toxic waste polluting the water;
and more generally the laws around property or land ownership, which favour the few at the expense of the many.
NGOs do not address this mismanagement at the state
level; instead, they try to compensate for it. 'Entrepreneurship' and 'independence' become the ultimate goals of
women's emancipation, privileging narratives of individual
achievement (as in the case of Khadija's co-op); rather than
demanding redress from the state for its failure, individuals
are expected to bear the responsibility of building structures to make up for where the state has failed. Terms like
'empowerment' are used to describe these projects, which
really only emphasize 'powerlessness' and corner women
into a narrative of victimhood. The mission of NGOs is
then to intervene in order to empower the victim and 'save
her', without taking into consideration the existing and
historical collective support networks among women —
especially among women farmers; this ill-considered intervention often risks breaking up these networks in order
to single out individuals and support them. These non-

Figure 4. The rock, the mountain, and the bullet. Author's photo.

governmental structures, functioning within the global capitalist economy, produce an apolitical managerial discourse that risks erasing the existing struggles of feminists.

THE ROCK. THE MOUNTAIN. THE BULLET.

On the border between Turkey, Iran, and Iraq, we are standing here on the Iraqi side of Kurdistan. Silence is quite heavy in these mountains and the speech act of the guerilla women from the Kurdish autonomous women's movement is the most powerful sound. It reverberates and echoes in the landscape. I interview many members of the movement there.

On the subject of self-defence — the core concept of the women's movement — I interviewed Dilar Dirik. She elaborates on this extralegality that is at the core of the struggle and the alliance between the women's movement and what she calls natural geographies, but also the intertwinement of ecological struggle, war, and emancipatory feminist politics:

> So self-defence actually comes from nature itself, it is something that is very organic and normal, every existence whether human or not relies on means of protecting itself. In the human context it cannot just be in the sense of the army or states or police or so on because they are very destructive systems which are not there to protect but which are there to kill and destroy.

> In liberalism, in liberal thought philosophy in general, the expectation [is] that people, groups, individuals should surrender the means of protection to the states, the states should have the monopoly on the use of force, and the assumption there is that you as an individual, as a member of society should not have the agency to act because the state should decide on your behalf what is dangerous to your existence, what is your existence to begin with.

> If we look at how nature organizes its self-defence we can draw from that a philosophy which is also ecological and which does not need to organize defence, to conquer, to objectify, to violate, to destroy another person, another group of people, another collective but rather, how can we in harmony within society, with other people, together make sure that we can survive, make sure that we can continue our existence and understand self-defence beyond the physical survival.

> Historically in the case of the Kurds, for example, the mountains have always been a very strong protector of the people who have been historically persecuted, also when in 2014 when ISIS attacked the Yazidis ... the first thing that they did was

> to flee to the mountains, or water or landscapes,
> natural geographies have always been sites of pro-
> tection of people and that is not because they are
> there in the service of humans but rather because
> humans are part of that region and humans have
> until the creation of big city-states and especially
> capitalism and industrialism people have always
> understood how to live together with nature, I
> know this for example from my own grandparents
> village, how they live and interact with nature,
> they have a very different relationship to the ani-
> mal[s] that they raise and very different relation-
> ship, they sing songs to the mountains, not about
> the mountains.

Another woman I met is the guerilla fighter Pelshin, who
is also one of the ideologues of the women's movement.
She serves on multiple committees; one of them is the
jineology committee (Kurdish for 'the study of women'),
which is a project to rewrite the history of science from
the perspective of women. The committee also publishes
a quarterly journal, Jineology. Thinking of different paradigms of communal life within the PKK and the relationship between knowledge, ideas, and practice, Pelshin
presents us with so many contradictory ideas and situations from guerila life. How to inhabit these contradic-
tions? Pelshin states:

> There is a contradiction between ecology and war.
> When I joined the guerrillas twenty-four years
> ago, I entered 'a war atmosphere'. The conditions
> were such that you sometimes needed to cut parts
> of trees, to have something to lie down on or to
> protect yourself from animals.
>
> The understanding of ecology in the women's
> movement was strongly influenced by these
> kind[s] of experiences and contradictions. Our
> ecological consciousness within the movement

evolved within our communal life in these conditions of war.

There's always a strong parallel between the massacre of nature and that of women. We, the women's movement, had to protect our existence.

I was in the mountains of Dersim for three years, where there are a lot of mountain goats. We were hungry many times during those three years, but only once did we kill goats for food. That is a rule of the guerilla.

I want to point out something about my personal experience. I remember my childhood. My first ecological teacher was my mother. She taught me that we as humans have a place in nature, like trees and birds. I have the right to exist, like all other species in the same place. You shouldn't hurt the earth, you should protect it. Don't kill trees, don't kill animals. But we are the children of the twentieth and twenty-first centuries, so it took a long time for this philosophy to reach us. But these things transmitted by my mother are the signs of this old philosophy.

Voiding is a carrier for ongoing violence, but also imbues destruction with the potential of communal visions and eco-feminist praxis. Ecological fragments and war-torn yet resistant murmurs of this atmospheric landscape made of sick fig trees, wild herbs, and medicinal plants; of rocks, mountains, and guerillas; and of bullets, fertilizers, and the NGOs show me how ideology is produced and practised on the ground.

Note the Ghosts
Among the More-than-Living in Iraq
KALI RUBAII

So many war-torn ecologies incorporate the kinds of more-than-humans that secular and Eurocentric discourse denies as existing or mattering by describing them as imaginaries or symbolic forms. From crocodile kin to the serpent who spawns fog, these different forms of existence refuse incorporation into vocabularies of Western theory.[1] For example, Marisol de la Cadena's book *Earth Beings* is based upon the author's moments of disconcertment that push the limits of political, environmental, and ontological understanding.[2]

Often classified as 'spiritual' or 'supernatural', these forces and beings are common arbiters of ecological (im)balance and mediators of malevolent/benevolent

---

1   Elizabeth Povinelli, *Geontologies: A Requiem for Late Liberalism* (Durham, NC: Duke University Press, 2016).

2   Marisol de la Cadena, *Earth Beings: Ecologies of Practice across Andean Worlds* (Durham, NC: Duke University Press, 2015).

relations between human beings and their environmental worlds. Sometimes they *are* the environment, as is the case of Turtle Island (North America) or Grandfather Crocodile (East Timor), and sometimes they are the sacred origin of human bodies, as is the case in Christianity.

Such beings are integral features of war-torn ecologies, which always incorporate more than simply the biomechanics of life-producing relations. Anyone who has lived among them knows that *non-living* more-than-humans are just as agentive as living ones — some, like heavy metals, cause cancer, while others, like minerals, are curative. They can also be more-than-material: ghosts, for example, are more-than-living but less-than-dead. They often haunt, warn, or physically injure.[3] Diné skinwalkers are transform. Brazilian umbanda requires a human host through incorporation. Sometimes non-living, non-material, more-than-humans seek revenge or rebalance.[4]

This is not to say that all people accept such forces are 'real', or that all cultures codify them as part of their ontology.[5] Certainly, many do not 'believe' in the encounters they experience, or the stories told by others because of this. Yet many do. Whether central to human narration, or ephemeral in their presence, these beings and forces

3   Sebastian Castelier and Quentin Muller, 'Gravediggers Claim Ghosts Haunt World's Largest Cemetery in Iraq', *Al Jazeera*, 10 September 2019 <https://www.aljazeera.com/features/2019/9/10/gravediggers-claim-ghosts-haunt-worlds-largest-cemetery-in-iraq> [accessed 12 November 2022].

4   See Farhan Ghanam, *Remaking the Modern: Space, Relocation, and the Politics of Identity in a Global Cairo* (Berkeley: University of California Press, 2002) on the Evil Eye's role in burning down businesses whose owners do not share with others.

5   Mayanthi L. Fernando, 'Supernatureculture', *The Immanent Frame*, 11 December 2017 <https://tif.ssrc.org/2017/12/11/supernatureculture/> [accessed 12 November 2022].

are important ones for understanding the affective components of ecological worlds, and for the political potential of collaboration or confrontation with them at the seams of violation and repair.

TOXIC AFFECTIVE ECOLOGIES OF WAR

At its points of combustion and along the tendrils of its underpinning economies, war makes atmospheres. War is an atmosphere. Nuclear tests go 'boom' once, but the world is never the same. Strontium in our teeth tells us so. So do Nadya's dreams, which make her wake up screaming years and years later. The fog of war is not always a fog. The uranium mined in Diné country toxified Diné people's bodies.[6] It also travelled. Maybe some of the same uranium reached Iraq in recent decades. Who knows, exactly? That is the point; specificities get diffused into the atmosphere. Some of those diffusions are ephemeral. Some are fixed.

In scholarship of the Middle East, the concept of 'war ecology' often refers to environments transformed by decades of intensive military violence. A war ecology is one shaped by war such that the interdependent webs by which new lives are made — and deaths are deemed meaningful — become fundamentally entangled with military remnants.

War ecologies preserve the scars of political violence.[7] They even give their own testimony. For example, babies born with birth defects in Iraq testify in their own unique way that, as Dr. Majid says, 'something is wrong here.'[8] If

---

6 Traci Brynne Voyles, *Wastelanding: Legacies of Uranium Mining in Navajo Country* (Minneapolis: University of Minnesota Press, 2015).

7 Omar Dewachi, *Ungovernable Life: Mandatory Medicine and Statecraft in Iraq* (Stanford, CA: Stanford University Press, 2019).

8 Kali Rubaii, 'Birth Defects and the Toxic Legacy of War in Iraq', *Middle East Report*, 296 (Fall 2020) <https://merip.org/2020/10/birth-

multinational corporations know the political trick 'dilu-
tion of pollution', then war's evidentiary ecologies of war
speak back.[9] They re-aggregate seemingly disparate phe-
nomena.

War has shaped Iraq's ecologies deeply. Many of the
Iraqis I spoke to during my fieldwork described enduring
environmental maladies, from plant crops and livestock
with malformed parts or tumorous growths to contaminated water. Perhaps most notorious as culprits are the
wastes of military base-making and post-war 'reconstruction': US burn-pits alone incinerated everything from ve-
hicles to computers.[10] Expended ordinances not only litter
the landscape, they are also circulated by people selling
the metal for a living. US military intervention in the early
2000s heavily damaged Iraq's diverse ecologies with an
onslaught of toxic inundation, compounding the toxic legacies of the Iran-Iraq War (1980–88) and the Gulf War
(1990–91). Toxic war materials are now embedded in
Iraq's landscape, and in the bodies of the thousands of
people living and dying with cancer, congenital anomal-
ies, asthma, and preventable infections. Toxins are similarly embedded in the water, air, and soil; and they travel
through exchanges of life-making processes across generations.

---

defects-and-the-toxic-legacy-of-war-in-iraq-296/> [accessed 12 November 2022].

9   Kristina Lyons, 'Chemical Warfare in Colombia, Evidentiary Ecol-
     ogies and Senti-actuando Practices of Justice', *Social Studies of
     Science*, 48.3 (June 2018), pp. 414–37 <https://doi.org/10.1177/
     0306312718765375>.

10   Kenneth MacLeish and Zoë H. Wool, 'US Military Burn Pits
     and the Politics of Health', *Medical Anthropology Quarterly*, 1 Au-
     gust 2018 <https://medanthroquarterly.org/critical-care/2018/08/
     us-military-burn-pits-and-the-politics-of-health/> [accessed 12 No-
     vember 2022].

But toxic legacies are not only material; they are also affective. What makes a place toxic? What makes a world unlivable, and what does it mean to be there nonetheless?

As depicted by Iraqi writers and poets like Sinan Antoon, Hassan Blasim, and Ahmed Saadawi, and by ethnographers like Hayder Al Mohammed, horror, mourning, and loss are central components in Iraq's affective ecologies. The following stories depict how toxic legacies haunt Iraq's landscapes, particularly for people repeatedly displaced by the material conditions of war.

If we generally recognize what a material substance is, then what is a toxic affect? These stories are non-fiction, based upon ethnographic interviews with Iraqi people in 2014 and 2015. Inclusive of actors like jinn and ghosts, who do not receive much credit for their participation in ecologies of war, these stories are testimonies to the diffuse forms of horror people confront as they live out the many forms of 'toxic' war.

NADYA'S DREAM ABOUT HER GHOST BABY (CONSTRUCTION SITE. MIRAWA, IRAQ. 2014)

> I crept up on you, squatting on the flat concrete slap, dusty from being new and unfinished. It makes you sneeze, very quietly, into the cheap, scratchy fabric of your sleeve. A shiver ran through you, in spite of the heat. Stagnant heat, thick for moving, thick enough to climb up, into the highest parts of the sky and then dive into, coming to a fast 'eeeeeerch'! Just above the floor. I think my dive pushed the air a little, and whisked out your fire. You cursed. You flicked the lighter, striking an orange glow for a second try. I squat right across from you. I blow a puff of air, like it is a birthday candle. I whisk the light out. It gives you the shivers, stagnant air that suddenly moves when you try to make a flame.

Do you remember, Mama, my first birthday party?
The candles were the kind that sparkle like little
firecrackers. You blow them out, and they light
back up again. Over and over and over. I wanted to
touch the flames, and you […] holding me back
while I squirmed against your arm, you laughed
so hard when you blew them out, and they came
right back up again. Your teeth were as white and
shiny as the moon. Those nights were hot nights.
July. We slept up on the roof, and the moon got so
bright, so round. You dropped a cloth over my face
to cover my eyes. I slept with my naked body out
in the night air, and my head covered. In the morning, when the sun was big like a blood orange, I
would crawl to Baba's legs — he slept with them
up like triangles — and lay down underneath in
the shade of his knees.

There is no roof on this house. It is unfinished. You
call it a construction site. The others call it a house.
Baba has called in some of his neighbours' debts.
Money is coming soon, and you will move to a
hotel. It will be cramped, but a fan will blow at
night. I cannot follow you there.

Shivers all the way down. That is the thing about
unfinished buildings like this. They are not already
filled with jinn. This one doesn't even have a roof.
But when you step out back to pour out a small
plastic bucket of dirty soapy water, after you wash
clothes and hang them on a wire outside, you
see something in the dried cement. A handprint.
Toddler size. When you gasp, I can feel part of
myself pulled into you. Your lungs make a squeeze,
and I struggle, tug, to pull myself out. You breathe
out a rattling sob. I escape you. Your chest aches.
You lay down to nap.

Mama, wake up and play with me. I climb the air
and free fall, making wind against your cheek. It
only soothes you in your sleep. So, I race through
the room knocking against things, but the sound is
mild. Your face is so tired, so hollowed out by loss.

I blow on the small flame you made, under the cooking pot. I blow and blow until a spark leaps off and scuttles across the concrete floor. It dies out. I blow and blow again, until more sparks fly. One single spark catches the hem of your abaya, down by your ankles.

I chase it, and blow softly. It kindles and grows, spreading a line of ember-orange like an infection, moving outward. It hits the stitching of gold, where a leaf is patterned into the side of the skirt to cover the seam of the side. The leaf blossoms into a flower, and makes the unfurling sound a flame makes when it breaks open at first. It does not wake you right away. Then it does, and you leap up, like a black flame yourself. You scream and stamp at the flower.

For a moment, the flame makes a wave of clear heat, and you stop everything, with large eyes. You can see me, my face, through the heat. You say my name like a question.

Then it is an emergency again. You reach toward the two plastic jugs in the corner — one for water, and one for fuel. You pour a jug over your head trying to put the fire out. Only, it is not water, it is fuel. The flame laps up the fluid like a ravenous cat. It consumes you. As the flower ignites your hair, you look calmly into my face. Then those bright white teeth appear. Is it a smile of joy, or the flames pulling the lips back from your face?

'Habibi', you say. 'My baby.'

As with so many toxins, like alcohol or fuel, this dusty air can transform the texture of a place. It can build atmospheres. A toxic relationship, a toxic environment, a toxic meal. Toxification renders harmful that which is essential to survival. Toxification makes certain places hostile, like the concrete walls that shelter and displace Nadya at the same time. Incomplete places are, after all, both inhospit-

able and a refuge. Nadya was not the only woman to warn
me of how hostile these incomplete dwellings could be,
even as she was deeply attached to remaining in this one.
Iraq's toxic ecology includes certain absent children, who
inhale and exhale 'brown breath.' They remain. They depart.
As do we.

THE JINN IN THE TOILET
(CONSTRUCTION SITE. MIRAWA, IRAQ. 2015)

> Don't go in there. That is a bathroom only for
> men now. We built a new pit for women on the
> other side. That one has a jinn. All these women
> in this house are suffering from it. Since the inva-
> sion, since 2003, there are many problems with
> reproduction. These women all have trouble with
> pregnancy. Me, I am a crone. I do not worry. But
> these are young ladies! They are married, and it is
> their joy to have children. They conceive, and even
> for a long time, they carry. And then, suddenly,
> there is a spontaneous abortion.

> So that bathroom in there […] a jinn crawled in
> and it waited. Each time there was an abortion,
> it took the blood and the clots and built a body
> for itself. It is a jinn made entirely of blood clots.
> It makes the 'toilet' bubble. It wants more blood,
> so it interferes, stealing phases from the women's
> cycles. If you go in that bathroom, everything will
> become erratic.

> One time the younger one, she was pregnant, very
> well. She went in that bathroom, and there was a
> rumbling in the pipe, and she felt the cold chill of
> that jinn around her. There was a loud noise, and
> she slipped off the bricks on the floor. She slipped
> and fell on her belly, and twisted her ankle. She fell
> so hard she lost the baby.

> Beware of that jinn, my dear. It steals children
> from women. But for the man, it is okay. It is safe.

The jinn is not interested in water or shit. It only builds itself out of blood clots, out of babies that are not full. So stay away, and go around to the other side of the house where it is safe.

The toxic is an immaterial force that makes its form out of bodies. Tumours. Cancers. It steals blood supplies. It takes flesh. It invades, outlasting people by consuming their bodies. War does not destroy everyone all at once. It takes time and moves slowly. Iraq's cancer rates are high. The rate of birth defects is high. Spontaneous abortions. Infertility. Things that make life travel across generations move under the shadow of an ongoing war. For so many, the echo, the shadow, is the main event. What does it mean to sit under the shade of these shadows, and to listen to these echoes?

THE GRAVEYARD
(ROUTE FROM SAQLAWIYA TO SULEYMANIA. 2015)

In Iraq, people visit graveyards. It is one of the places where things make sense, where the ghosts and the sorrow can be aired, where the suffering can be allowed to breathe. The poet Sinan Antoon jostled my elbow once at a talk in New York, 'Iraq needs some time for the ghosts to breathe'. I like Sinan for embracing a period of necessary negativity. He reminds me of Frantz Fanon a little bit.

Now, Hameed and I are alone. We have hustled through the checkpoints and the dusty road. We replaced a punctured car tire on the side of the long, straight highway. We made it to his village. And we have done this magical thing he taught me: fertilizing a date flower by inducing it to nectar with an onion. I have never seen a flower cry like a human eye, but it did. The way men cry when they are trying to be masculine, wet and nearly overflowing. Not a trickling line, or anything close to a torrent. It was enough. The pollen stuck to the stamen. The dates might just make it, if they are given the chance to fruit.

Now we are driving away from the date plantation, back toward Kirkuk. The booming sound of war is so faint it might just be my memory making me think I can still hear it. That is, maybe, what a ghost feels like.

One stop, on the way back across the dry landscape. Here, past a simple hump of dirt, is a small graveyard. I love Muslim graveyards. They often do not mark names and dates, or use marble headstones. They are simple rocks, marking the presence of a body, working hard to unmoor the index of a thing from the thing itself. This is a headstone, not a person. This is an image of a thing, not the thing itself. There is no mistaking the material thing for what it is meant to index.

Hameed kneels down by a stone. He visits someone regularly here. I notice that he has headed toward the smaller graves.

There are graves for so many little people. That is, in the end, the real echo of war. The cholera. The diarrhoea. The meningitis. The miscarriages. The heart defects. The asthma. All treatable things under ordinary conditions. All deaths. 'Maybe some of the children here were shot', Hameed says. 'But I don't think so. That is not how war usually kills children. It does it more like torture. From sicknesses and slower things.'

He does not touch the stones. I can see from his hands that he wants to, but he hesitates. He takes his tentative, earthen hands from where they hover over the stones, and instead places them formally, like a soldier acting out a duty, in the shape of an open book. Palms up. Palms slanted inward. And as he recites a passage of the Quran, I look off into the distance, trying to be respectful of his private ache.

I see rows of wheat. I see black smoke from a distant oil refinery. I see the land ebbing into a faint green where the Euphrates curves in the distance. I see green, but that is just the index of the thing itself. I do not see the water. It is not the green I love, Hameed reminds me, it is the water the green tells me is there…

'What are you doing?' He catches me staring away. His palms break their magnetic hold on each other, and open up a wide space. He is making a room for me to step through. He is gesturing like a butler to the hallway of stones, lined up one after the other. 'Bear witness!' he says in English, then turns back to his prayer.

I walk like a reluctant voyeur past each stone. I take in the graveyard. I step through small prickles of dead grass Velcro-ing themselves to my ankles. I stop suddenly. I think I hear a strange laugh and feel a small, playful presence behind me. I turn, half expecting to see a creature like a fox or a rodent. I see nothing.

I walk on, trying to focus on the sombre alignment of graves. 'These are children!' I hear myself think in an emphatic whisper. But my sobriety is irked by the presence of something impish behind me, breathing on me, making the feeling of laughter ring in my head. I am annoyed and turn quickly this time, hoping to catch the glimpse of the trickster child behind me. (I am sure there will be a little boy who has popped out from somewhere, curious and giggling.) I am ready to be asked for money. But again, no one is there. I am absolutely certain this time that I felt something tugging on my skirt. Hameed's eyes are still closed. He is in mourning. I do not know for whom or how many we have stopped here.

I turn to the place in the air where I feel a presence. 'I feel you. I know you are there. Please leave me alone. I am trying to be sad.' I say it in a whisper,

not wanting Hameed to think I am hallucinating.
But, as if in answer, I feel the smack of moving
air against me and am overcome by a giddy, rising
laughter. I cannot contain it. It bursts out of me,
using my lungs for its own exodus. I am laughing
so hard I keel over, with my hands on my knees.

I can see the scene from outside of myself: an Iraqi-
American woman cracking up in the middle of a
sea of small baby graves. It is a hideous scene. I
am embarrassed. Hameed calls the laughter 'dry
crying', and doesn't seem to think it is strange.

'What was that?' I ask him in the car as we drive
on.

'Maybe it was a ghost. But I am a pious man. I
only believe in God.' He winks. I know Hameed
believes in ghosts.

'Did you mean to introduce me to it?'

'Maybe', he winks, again.

'Was it your child?'

'Does it matter?'

(A little! I think.) I study the side of his face. 'Yes.
It matters.'

'Good.' He tilts his back on the driver's seat head-
rest, which is covered in a mesh of wooden beads.
He looks satisfied.

To recognize is not enough. Solidarity might require more. My body overtaken by another, just
a little; Hameed introducing me to something,
or someone, but not fully acknowledging it; the
movement of air against and through me. I am
no longer bearing witness; I am the technology
of a ghost. Hameed is repurposing my form, or
rather, offering me up for repurposing. I came, I
said, to bear witness. But bearing such witness un-
wittingly pushed laughter that is not laughter out
of me. The ecology of affects is [...] toxic.

THE PILLOW STORY, BY YOUNG DINA: PART I
(DOHUK. 2014)

It is easy to imagine the sound of a heartbeat. You can just listen to your own. When we were more alive, more connected to things, the sound of my own heartbeat was the only thing I feared. Now, Ya Allah, it is the only thing I don't fear.

When I was very little, before I met you, I was afraid to lay my head down on my pillow. Each time I did, I heard the merciless crunch, crunch, crunch of many tiny little elves with many tiny pickaxes, hacking away at the snowbank of my pillow. They were digging their way up, trying to escape from underneath the weight of my head. I knew they suffered when I lay my head down, because if I pressed my ear softly over the pillow and suspended the weight of my skull, the sound of their labour diminished. I feared that if I fell asleep, they would succeed in the night, hack through the pillow, and climb into my ear.

I used to worry the elves would whistle while they worked, just like in the cartoon about the seven dwarves. If I let them tunnel through my pillow and climb one by one, hand over hand, into my ear […] then the whistling of their work and the stabbing pain of their picks and the feeling of something in my ear would make me crazy. I would run around screaming like the old woman in our neighbourhood who lost her mind when they delivered her son back to her drooling and incontinent from electric shock torture. But that was in Saddam Time. Now the sons are born this way from the start. Or, if they are healthy, they are hunted by militias and stripped of their IDs and jobs and even their high school diplomas.

I am a girl, so I have to worry about losing my mind. I heard them talk about this on the British media channel. They call it trauma. They say most children in Iraq saw family members murdered before they turned ten. They say that we cannot plan the future. We cannot concentrate in school. We cannot sleep through the night. But I never planned, I never concentrated in school, and I never ever slept through the night. Those little elves were trying to break through my pillow, and my father always tells me that you are only paranoid if you are wrong, so I would stay up as long as I could, until long after the adults were snoring.

One morning, men broke through the front door instead of my pillow. They dragged my mum outside and arrested her. They said they would keep the women in prison until the men agreed to end their protests. My father said that protest was a democratic right. The police officer, who was holding my mother, spat on the floor of our house. My father told me it is rude to spit, even if you have sand in your mouth.

My father sent a lot of letters to different ministries in Baghdad, but my mother never came home. Um Ahmed brings us food from next door. Sometimes her granddaughter brings it over. Her granddaughter is very quiet and very shy. My father tells me not to be shy or quiet. Giving up a voice you have is like giving up a vote you are entitled to.

Um Ahmed has maybe been a widow since the war with Iran. Her husband went missing and was never returned, so my mother said to never call her a widow. But she is probably a widow. We don't say it, though. My father calls that an 'open secret', and says that open secrets are dangerous. But my mother said open secrets are how women get men to act decently, and that keeping people's secrets is polite. I am polite, so I don't call my father a widower even though my mother is missing. And I never tell anyone that there is a small army of little elves trying to hack their way through my pillow every night. They are fast. Whenever I lift the pillow, they are gone. Even though my father says that 'eyes believe themselves and ears believe other people', he also doesn't agree with keeping secrets, so I am not sure. Maybe when we hear something, it is enough to know it is coming for us.

A toxic affect both warns and erases. It makes a nest out of absences, uncertainties, and anxieties. That which is unseen has its affects precisely because of this. Affect, after all, is known without being seen; felt without verification. A toxic affect evades a gaze, skips across time…

THE PILLOW STORY, BY YOUNG DINA: PART II (DOHUK. 2015)

You are back to visit! I got a little older, see? I experimented in the past years, trying to find the little elves in my pillow. My father gave me a stethoscope for my birthday, even though I never told him about the elves. He says I will be a doctor like my mother. I discovered that the little men pickaxing rhythmically in my pillow are actually my heartbeat pounding in my head. I discovered that it is possible to hear blood rushing in my body.

Bombs. They shrieked like the crazy old woman in the neighbourhood whose son came home drooling and incontinent. The first one I ever heard, I thought it was a phoenix. It sounded like a phoenix. It burned like one, too. It made a building in the distance puff up in smoke. But then my father shouted at us, 'Bombs! Get down!' He remembered them from the US war. I didn't remember any wars. 'You do now', he said.

This kind of war is called 'civil'. We put all our documents in a folder and I got to pick out a dress and three of my favourite books. We also put some food in a big sheet with a flashlight and a blanket. When we ran away from the phoenix, my father looked like an old cartoon character of a peddler with a bundle on his back. I held on to his belt loop so I wouldn't get lost. Everyone was moving like animals being hunted. I saw all the people, my neighbours, but they did not stop to say hello. My mother says it is not polite to go past without saying hello, so I stopped and tried to be polite. No one seemed to hear me. My father said we were in a hurry and this was a special circumstance. Life-and-death is a special circumstance.

We travelled for a long time, and stayed with friends and family on the way out of our home. I saw places I have never seen! The river is wide, but the desert is wider. It opens up like a gaping plane and it does not have many tall buildings or many plants. I forget the colour green. I forget the smell of water. I forget feeding the animals.

And then, we are in a new place. I know it is a new place because we are not connected to things. We reach the limit of my father's realm. He does not shake hands and kiss the men driving the cabs, or the storeowners. They do not know him, and they do not know anyone who knows him. We cannot call out our family name and find someone to answer. We are ghareeb, strangers. When you are ghareeb, my father says, you need money to make things happen. When you are connected, more alive, you do not. Even now, people speak a different language. They speak Arabic, too, but also Kurdish. We do not speak Kurdish. When we open our mouths or show our faces, we show we are ghareeb.

I feel sorry for the big families, with so many people not-missing and not-dead who need a place to be and food to eat and water to drink. We have a little money. It is enough to buy a tooth-brush and toothpaste. My father says that my teeth are very important. I am growing adult teeth, and I have to take extra care of them. Without teeth, you cannot eat. 'Baba, we need food to eat, too!' We have enough money for food. We find a mosque for sleep. At the mosque there is always a toilet, a washroom, and a place to lie down and rest.

It is just my father and me. He tells me a heart has only so many beats, to use them wisely. When the time is up, it is up. I wonder how many beats my mother's heart has. When is it time to call my father a widower? Can a person be more alive and less alive, or is it a final moment, a last beat?

This mosque will not allow me to go in with my father on the men's side. My father calls it 'fanaticism' to expect that little girls live by the restrictions of women. My mother called it fanaticism to expect women to live by the restrictions of women. But these are special circumstances. My father gives up the voice he has. The women staying in the mosque take me with them to the other side. Some of the women wear all black from head to toe. They keep their heads covered even outside of the mosque.

My father is on the other side of a wall, and I sleep on the floor in the mosque as close to that wall as I can. One of the women snores very loudly. I am ghareeb all the way down. I am not connected to anything. I am just one single body with no ties.

When I laid my head directly on the floor to sleep, a chill of fear ran through me. There was no sound of elves with pickaxes chipping away at the snowy down of my pillow. There was no pillow!

It makes sense. My father says that destroying a habitat destroys a people. In Saddam Time they destroyed the habitat of the marsh in the south. In Maliki Time, they destroyed the city of Fallujah and sent us scattering like bugs into Kurdistan. They also destroyed my pillow and sent the elves away.

I know they are not really elves. They say the thing you fear now is the thing you will miss later. It is true! I know that the sound I miss is the sound of

> my own heartbeat. This terrifies me much more than the fear that little elves might crawl into my ear while I sleep. I am not connected to things, even those little things that might tickle me or cause me pain or drive me crazy, like the woman whose son was returned to her drooling and incontinent.
>
> I cannot hear my own heartbeat.
>
> This is a special circumstance: I am less alive.

When destroying a habitat destroys a people, ghareeb appears as a toxic affect. For Dina, ghareeb is realized through an encounter with herself as she becomes disconnected, isolated, less a part of the landscape than before, along with those in her life. Absence becomes the condition of possibility for existence.

TOXIC AFFECTS

Ecologies of war are packed with living and non-living beings, with less-living beings and with more-than-living beings. 'Brown breath' rises from the floor of a mosque, from a graveyard, from the pillow, the toilet, and from the construction site. These sites of refusal and belonging are thresholds at the precipice of the vital, charged with intense and incommensurable feelings that make up the affective ecology of war.

War-torn ecologies cannot be reduced to relations of reproduction. The living manage relationships with a toxic war ecology through the atmospherics of everyday life, atmospherics shaped by the force of elves and jinn, ghosts and laughing breezes. These are the toxic affects of war, easily invisible or left to whispers or glances, hidden where they like to be, at the margins of the speakable. Toxic affects play tricks. They sap life. They take flesh. They give feeling.

They evade capture. They insist upon meaning for those lives which have been otherwise undermined as meaningless.

Note the ghosts. Anyone who has lived among them knows that *non-living* more-than-humans are agentive and powerful, affecting the quality, tone, and texture of meaning. They are fundamentally ecological, because they are infused in the relations and processes of making new kinds of lives by and through thick intimacies. Living in a war ecology necessitates building upon these intimacies, because they are embedded into the potential of survival.

Whether central to human narration, or ephemeral in their presence, these beings and forces are important ones for understanding the affective components of ecological worlds, and for the political potential of collaboration or confrontation with them at the seams of violation and repair.

Great Sand

Grains of Occupation and Representation

NADINE HATTOM

> We can't deny that the landscapes
> we produce are embodied
> within the identities we assume.

THE SEARCH, PART I: IRAQ

In 2013, I drove through the Syrian Desert in Jordan toward the Iraq border. It would be the closest I could get to Iraq in the twenty-five years since leaving. I stopped some sixty kilometres short of the border; the taxi driver was anxious to turn back. I took a photograph of the sprawling desert with my medium-format camera — a landscape image that would come to represent a long investigation into how landscapes of heritage and imagination shape our identities.

As I was researching the journey to the Jordanian–Iraqi border, I searched online for landscape images of Anbar Province in Iraq. I wanted to see what the area looked like. I was confronted with an overwhelming number of images of the US military occupation of Iraq.

Military images dominated the online presence and furthermore, were included in cultural heritage documentation as visual material. It was as though the place didn't exist without militarization. The very-high resolution images were predominantly from the US Department of Defense archive documenting Operation Iraqi Freedom and the Iraq War of 2003. The archive contained thousands of images by military personnel detailing activities and missions.

Knowing that this land existed without occupation and feeling that this representation was an injustice, I was compelled to reveal the beauty of the landscape and re-move the occupier. So I digitally removed the soldiers from a selection of images from the archive, approximating the space they occupied. It soon became clear, however, that I could never erase or undo what took place in the landscape, and I decided to leave the soldiers' shadows in the earth, as a trace of the long shadow that war has left behind. In the words of James Joyce, 'places remember events.' This remembrance is imprinted in the earth itself, albeit ephem-erally.

In removing the soldiers I intervened in the landscape, resisted its militarization, and reframed its representation. I also became aware that by removing the figures in the landscape, the real subject of the image was revealed — that which was projected onto the land itself. An assump-tion about an entire region.

The work 'Shadows' is a series of ten digitally modified photographs from the Department of Defense Operation

Figure 1: 'U.S. Marines of Company G, 2nd Battalion, 2nd Marines, fall into a tactical column as they maneuver through a palm grove to conduct a security patrol in Fallujah, Iraq, on Oct. 22, 2005. DoD photo by Sgt. Paul S. Mancuso, U.S. Marine Corps. (Released)'

Iraqi Freedom archive.[1] Each photograph is accompanied by a caption that describes what is happening in the image and who took it, providing a look into the language of warfare in the public domain. See for example the caption of Figure 1.

Militarizing a landscape involves defining and being defined by processes that result in the space being read

---

1   See the page 'Shadows' (13 July 2017) on my website <http://nadinehattom.com/shadows/> [accessed 12 November 2022].

as militarized.[2] 'Military control over space is as much a strategic task of representation as it is a physical act.'[3]

At the very least, Operation Iraqi Freedom's processes consisted of 'weapons searches', 'security patrols', 'area scans', 'beach insertions along lake shores', and 'disruption operations'. Combat artillery and barracks coupled with a presence in uniform, form an act of occupation.

But an archive of images documenting these acts disguises a total occupation of a people's history and their right to exist on their own terms. As Judith Butler writes, describing Susan Sontag's famous critique of war photography, 'the photograph substitutes for the event to such an extent that it structures memory more effectively than either understanding or narrative.'[4]

Beyond occupation with a physical presence, this archive of images serves to occupy the narrative of the war and legitimize violence. But what I saw in these high-resolution images was a palette of sandy beiges, sunburnt greens, and high-noon blues that tell a far different story.

So, where is the archive that writes a history of what really took place in this landscape?

THE SEARCH, PART II: GERMANY

While researching another trip for a different project, this time in Germany, I was looking for sand. Specifically, a sandy, inland landscape, perhaps with dunes. A landscape

---

2   Matthew Flintam, 'Parallel Landscapes: A Spatial and Critical Study of Militarised Sites in the United Kingdom' (PhD diss., Royal College of Art, 2010).

3   Rachel Woodward, 'How Military Landscapes Work', in *Military Landscapes*, ed. by Ingrid Book and Carina Heden (Bergen: Bergen Kunsthalle, 2008), pp. 78–101 (p. 81).

4   Judith Butler, *Frames of War: When Is Life Grievable?* (London: Verso, 2016), p. 71.

to approximate what I know and relate to — namely, a desert landscape.

Deserts don't exist in Germany, whose geography consists of temperate forests, lakes, rivers, and mountains. However, near Mainz, in Germany's southwest, is a sandy expanse, a relic from the last ice age called the Großer Sand, or Great Sand. The sand there consists of calcareous sediment from the Rhine riverbed that was transported by the wind to the northern slopes of the Rhenish Hesse plateau around twenty thousand years ago.[5]

The Great Sand is a nature reserve on an area of only 1.27 square kilometers and a habitat to a multitude of endangered flora, some on the verge of extinction. Around ten thousand years ago, steppe plants from western Asia and southeastern Europe migrated to the dunes, followed by plants from the Mediterranean. According to the Johannes Gutenberg Universität Mainz website, 'it is the only area in Central Europe that has been able to retain this character thanks to the particular local conditions.'

How is it that this landscape continues to exist and resist the dominant vegetation? Part of the answer is that this landscape has been occupied by militaries since the eighteenth century. First by French troops of the First French Republic (1799–1804) and the First French Empire (1804–14), followed by Prussian troops, Austrian troops, the Wehrmacht, the French again, and finally, the United States Army, which is still present there today.[6]

---

5   Johannes Gutenberg-Universität Mainz, 'The Mainz Sand Dunes Landscape', last modified 5 January 2012 <https://www.botgarden.uni-mainz.de/outdoor-grounds/the-mainz-sand-dunes-landscape/> [12 November 2022].

6   Wikipedia, s.v. 'Grosser Sand', (in German), last modified 18 September 2020 <https://de.wikipedia.org/wiki/Gro%C3%9Fer_Sand>.

The military presence involved the diligent removal of trees and bushes to provide a clearing for artillery training. The 24th Military Intelligence Battalion of the 66th Military Intelligence Brigade is one of the United States Army Europe (USAREUR) units currently using the sand dunes local training area. Since its activation on 15 July 2009 in the Mainz Sand Dunes, the unit has supported operations including Operation Iraqi Freedom (Iraq), Operation New Dawn (Iraq 2010–11, Afghanistan), Operation Enduring Freedom (global war on terror), and Operation Unified Protector (Libya).[7] The 66th Military Intelligence Brigade has also been associated with the atrocities committed at the Abu Ghraib detention facility.[8]

Despite protests against the nature reserve being used as a military training area and skepticism about how closely the area resembles the landscapes that it is supposed to simulate, such as Afghanistan, USAREUR continues to train for combat there.[9]

When I searched online for images of the Great Sand near Mainz, I found that stock photographs featured prominently. The photographs document the US military's training activities. Figure 2 shows a stock image with caption.

The photographs bear a strong resemblance to the Department of Defense (DoD) archive images of Operation Iraqi Freedom although the landscapes are worlds apart

---

7   66th Military Intelligence Battalion website, last modified 26 July 2018
     <https://www.inscom.army.mil/msc/66mib/24thMI.html>.
8   George R. Fay, 'Investigation of the Abu Ghraib Detention Facility
     and 205th Military Intelligence Brigade MG', 2004, p. 43 <https://
     www.thetorturedatabase.org/document/fay-report-investigation-
     205th-military-intelligence-brigades-activites-abu-ghraib>.
9   Ludger Fittkau, 'Kampftraining im Naturschutzgebiet: Kriegsübungen
     der US-Army im Mainzer Sand lösen Protest aus', Deutschlandradio,
     31 May 2012, 14:17:31–14:23:09 (no longer online, but available upon
     request from Deutschlandradio Archiv).

Figure 2: 'Soldiers assigned to 24th Military Intelligence Battalion, 66th Military Intelligence Brigade, conduct a Land Navigation Course during the Best Warrior Competition in the Sand Dunes Training Area located in Mainz, Germany, 28 March, 2017. The competition put its candidates through a series of physical and mental challenges including marksmanship; physical fitness; day and night land navigation; tactical communications; medical aid; board appearances and written exams; weapons skills; obstacle course negotiation; a 12-mile foot march; and a battery of other Soldier tasks and drills. U.S. Army.'

and do not look alike. However, the composition of the photographs and the relationship between the subject (the soldiers) and their surroundings (a sandy landscape) are strikingly similar. The high sun casts shadows and gives a distinctive hue to the foliage and the golden sand. The soldiers strike active poses that anticipate violence.

The photographs conjure a sense of a staged performance, blurring the lines between the real and the imagined. What is the difference between simulated and real warfare in these images? It can't be found in either image. Presented with both, one risks concluding that these are natural scenarios. However, I insist that both are carefully composed and manufactured with intent. They document neither actual combat nor the simulation in a landscape that contains the elements that mark it as suitable for war.

The problem is, nonetheless, that the photographs serve to legitimize both scenarios by their being indistinguishable and therefore natural. Moreover, photography has long been perceived to assert truth: indeed, it 'is built into the case made for truth ... there can be no truth without photography'.[10]

Once this truth is established and accepted, it forms a basis for further acts that take this truth as a starting point. And the result is a war that is manufactured, mass produced, and exported.

My search came to an end. Once again I had sought a landscape that I identify with, and again I found that it was occupied.

SHIFTING SANDS

What builds the case for militarizing a landscape? Which elements provide a space that invites militarization?

The Great Sand has many aspects that speak for the case against assuming it as a military training ground, including its size and its status as a nature reserve with endangered flora. But there seems to have been one very compelling reason for USAREUR to establish a presence there.

---

10   Butler, *Frames of War*, p. 70.

After all, it is one of very few areas in Germany that provide a sandy landscape. Perhaps the most obvious place to start is with the name, the Great Sand. Sand is its defining characteristic. Is the presence of sand, however small in proportion — the Great Sand is a mere 1.27 square kilometres — enough to serve as a surface on which to project conflict and thus to militarize? To convince as a place to produce and reproduce war?[11] As one scholar observes, it is 'no longer possible to treat landscape and war as separate realms. Instead, the challenge is to explore how war and landscapes reciprocally reproduce each other across time and space.'[12]

Perhaps the Great Sand acts as a sand table. Like Reisswitz's prototype of the original *Kriegsspiel* (war game), in which a table topped with damp sand served as an effective surface to project conflict and play out war games, transforming the sand into any landscape.

What would happen if you replaced sand with soil? Sandy paths with mud? Grass with dense forest? Would that change the nature of the conflict? Would it perhaps even shift the conflict to an entirely different region? The elements of the landscape have geopolitical implications. If you could imbue a grain of sand with a different set of associations, if you could stage an intervention that completely transformed the landscape, would the space continue to serve as a legitimate site for the production of combat?

In choosing a military training area, would an open landscape based on soil be too familiar? Does sand serve

---

11   Zoltan Grossman, 'War and New US Military Bases', *CounterPunch*, 2 February 2002 <https://www.counterpunch.org/2002/02/02/war-and-new-us-military-bases/> [accessed 12 November 2022].

12   Chris Pearson, 'Researching Militarized Landscapes: A Literature Review on War and the Militarization of the Environment', *Landscape Research*, 37.1 (2012), pp. 115–33.

to transport and thus manufacture a fantasy on which to project aggression?

It takes a landscape which has the characteristics of a 'foreign' territory, an 'elsewhere' on which to project conflict. Do sand dunes conjure this imagination?

'Military landscapes are constructed with intent. The assertion of future intentionality to continue to shape such spaces in the military's image confirms that right to be.'[13] These landscapes have to continue to produce the need for militarization in order to preserve the military's stronghold on the space. What if a 'foreign' landscape exists within our midst but is part of the fabric of our collective identities? This foreignness doesn't immediately call for militarization or a show of aggression or force.

The Great Sand is also not the only inland sand dune in Europe used for this purpose. The inland dune in Jüterbog, Germany, another relic of the last ice age, was used as a military training area for 150 years — and until 1994 by the Soviets. More examples include the Biville Dunes in France, Braunton Burrows in the UK, Drift Sand Nature Reserve in the Netherlands, and Záhorie Sands in Slovakia.

Researcher Rachel Woodward notes that there is a core idea among national military forces that 'certain iconic types of landscape, that inform widely-shared national cultures of identity, are suitable and somehow naturally appropriate for military use'.[14] Perhaps the idea is connected to certain landscapes that need to be 'conquered' or present some particular physical or mental challenge. But because soldiers are shaped by and in turn shape the landscape — 'The soldier is made in military landscapes, and military landscapes impact upon the

---

13   Woodward, 'How Military Landscapes Work', p. 84.
14   Ibid., p. 81.

soldier'[15] — a narrative of dominance must be inserted into the landscape for this process to work. The space itself is not separate from the act of soldiers becoming and thus carrying out acts that militarize the space.

In other words, 'the projection of military power in a landscape is reliant on the legitimation of spaces — how it is framed and represented — through which this can happen.'[16] Legitimizing the space can't take place irrespective of what elements are present within it. It relies on perhaps just a few key pieces in order for the narrative to be successful. This 'framing and representation' is then exported to an entire region.

The landscapes we choose to project our conflicts onto have an impact on the warfare we readily engage in and the conflicts we devise as a result.[17] Furthermore, they have a lasting effect on the narratives associated with the space and the elements within it.

An example from the Alps in the World War I illustrates how a militarized landscape can have a profound impact on ways of understanding the landscape and in turn the people for whom this landscape forms an integral part of their culture. The war transformed the once peaceful realm of solitude and escape into the military 'bulwark of the nation'.[18] The peaks, once a source for an ideology of freedom and spirituality, could no longer be seen the way they were before they were militarized; their meaning was redefined. They even imparted new meaning to activities

---

15   Ibid., p. 96.
16   Henrik Strömsten, 'Military and Nature: An Environmental History of Swedish Military Landscapes' (MA thesis, Uppsala University, 2016), p. 10.
17   Grossman, 'War and New US Military Bases'.
18   Tait Keller, 'The Mountains Roar: The Alps during the Great War', *Environmental History*, 14.2 (2009), pp. 253–74 (p. 253).

not formerly associated with conflict, as they 'diminished the distinction between mountain climbers and combatants'.[19] Which is to say that to exist in the landscape, meant to become militarized.

We can take a closer look at the 66th Military Intelligence Brigade for hints of how the perception of the so-called desert landscape is entwined with the production of conflict. The brigade has been active in Germany since 1968, with its mission to provide intelligence for USAREUR 'in order to facilitate the gaining and maintaining of information dominance'.[20] Their shoulder sleeve insignia includes a sphinx and is described on its website as 'an oriental blue hexagon bearing a yellow sphinx superimposed by a silver gray dagger hilted black'. The distinctive unit insignia also includes a sphinx and is described as 'composed of a chequy of nine sections of Gold and Blue (oriental) with the center square charged with a Gold sphinx head'. The detail 'oriental' blue is intriguing, as it is the less common name for ultramarine blue: 'The name comes from the Latin *ultramarinus*, literally "beyond the sea," because the pigment was imported into Europe from mines in Afghanistan by Italian traders during the 14th and 15th centuries.'[21] A deliberate use of an uncommon name for ultramarine blue.

To what extent is the idea of an oriental, desert sand landscape coupled with the imagining of warfare? The oriental blue coupled with the Sphinx of Giza was chosen as a specific image to use as an emblem for exercising force.

19   Ibid., p. 270.

20   66th Military Intelligence Battalion website <https://www.inscom. army.mil/msc/66mib/24thMI.html>.

21   Wikipedia, s.v. 'Ultramarine', last modified 19 April 2021 <https://en. wikipedia.org/wiki/Ultramarine>.

Figure 3. Shoulder sleeve insignia (left) and distinctive unit
insignia (right) of the 66th Military Intelligence Brigade.

There is also often a link between conservation and
military landscapes. This association forms a part of the
narrative of legitimation of the space, and also serves the
perception that the military is there to 'defend'. In the case
of nature conservation, then, the military wants to 'defend'
the landscape from either invasive species or human inter-
ference. 'Military land use is legitimated through strategies
of naturalization.'[22]

In the case of the Great Sand, the US Army reported in
2009 that it served to protect the Great Sand nature reserve,
that its presence was therefore beneficial, perhaps crucial
to conservation, and that through 'close cooperation with
German authorities' it had conducted 'a Threatened and
Endangered Species survey in 2007'. The survey indicated
that 'encroaching urban development, resulting pollution
and the abundance of Black Locust Trees planted in the
eastern part of the installation were all leading to a dramatic
shift in the soil makeup and ecological diversity'. The army
then led an initiative to remove invasive trees and bushes

---

22   Woodward, 'How Military Landscapes Work', p. 81.

(the Black Locust Tree is native to North America), claiming that 'U.S. Army environmentalists and training support providers are living up to the Defense Department's motto of being good stewards of the earth wherever Soldiers are called upon to serve.'[23]

Do we need to militarize a landscape in order to conserve the planet and protect it from 'encroaching urban development, resulting pollution'? Are these the best conditions for wildlife to thrive, the most 'original' state?

The military maintains this unique geography through its activity, but in doing so also ensures that it remains a militarized landscape. It follows that this militarized and thus conserved landscape must not contain humans. If it does, then the only humans permitted there are those who are trained to kill other humans in order to eliminate them from this and similar landscapes.

'For all national military forces, ideas about national identity are implicit within military representations of landscape, and complicit in their construction.'[24]

How the chosen military training landscape then shapes the national identity perpetuated by the military shapes the national identity of the wider population.

So, why does it matter if a particular landscape or a specific feature of that landscape is militarized?

First, it matters to the people in the regions that conflict is being exported to. Operation Iraqi Freedom, Operation New Dawn, Operation Enduring Freedom, and Operation Unified Protector are all conflicts in regions that are associated with this landscape. The identities of the people in these regions are inextricably linked to a sandy

---

23   Karl Weisel, 'Project Serves Soldiers and the Environment', US Army website, 23 February 2009 <https://www.army.mil/article/17299/ project_serves_soldiers_and_the_environment>.

24   Woodward, 'How Military Landscapes Work'.

landscape, built through experiences in their surroundings. Memories and histories are made against the backdrop of particular colours, smells, and textures. The landscape shapes how people relate to their environment and this in turn forms the idea and delineation of what that landscape is.

Second, it matters to the places that contain these numerous militarized areas. They are among nations that may not believe they have much to do with the conflicts going on 'over there'. Training areas make up approximately 6 percent of the earth's land mass.[25] A military training area next door doesn't mean that we are separate from what takes place there or that it doesn't affect us. It is part of the fabric of the entire landscape that surrounds us. This means that not only the whole landscape but the whole culture encompasses those activities. A conflict takes place both 'over there' and on our doorstep. The conflict abroad is in fact mirrored in the very landscape that the military claims to protect.

> [L]andscape can be understood with reference to the representational qualities of landscapes, an approach which understands landscapes as texts to be read for what they tell us about the exercise of power over space. Third, landscapes are also experiential, engaged with through bodies, senses, movements and emotions, and brought into being through our being.[26]

25   Rick Zentelis and David Lindenmayer, 'Bombing for Biodiversity —
      Enhancing Conservation Values of Military Training Areas', *Conserva-
      tion Letters*, 8.4 (July/August 2015), pp. 299–305 <https://doi.org/10.
      1111/conl.12155>.

26   Rachel Woodward, 'Military Landscapes: Agendas and Approaches for
      Future Research', *Progress in Human Geography*, 38.1 (February 2014),
      pp. 40–61 (p. 41) <https://doi.org/10.1177/0309132513493219>.

Our reading of landscapes reveals the narratives that we have embedded within them. It reveals that landscapes form an integral part of who we are and that we are not separate from them or from the processes that produce them. People whom we classify as belonging to that place, and those who identify with it are as much a part of that narrative.

As we militarize certain elements, like sand, marking a sandy landscape as a stage for warfare, we also occupy the imagination that takes this landscape as inspiration. For entire regions this is an occupation of the people's agency over their own representation.

To demilitarize and decolonize sand requires a different narrative that will become as ubiquitous as the material itself, one that is no longer associated with violence and war but simply with life there, in all its richness.

Hide Your Water from the Sun
A Performance for Spirited Waters
JUMANA EMIL ABBOUD

The following is a selection from an ongoing journal I began keeping in 2010. This particular selection was written as part of a performance I presented at the Khalil Sakakini Cultural Center in 2016. Together with photographer Issa Freij, I sought to find the sites that were once believed to have been enchanted by supernatural beings — beings who possessed the natural springs, wells, and streams. Promising to guard the waters, the spirits inspired valuable practices around natural resources and harnessed a unique relationship with the land through unbounded time.[1]

We are following them: their tracks are hard to find, often buried.

---

1   Some material used in this performance was originally published in Jumana Emil Abboud, *In aching agony and longing I wait for you by the Spring of Thieves*, ed. by Lara Khaldi (London: Black Dog Press, 2018). The folktales presented here are revised versions of those found in Ibrahim Muhawi and Sharif Kanaana, *Speak Bird Speak Again: Palestinian Arab Folktales* (Berkeley: University of California Press, 1989).

There are sounds we do not recognize: wind howls, echoes of children calling out from a distance. The quietness of the landscape untouched by criminality.

Beit-Illu, Ein Zarqa, Kobar, deir Ghassana, Bir Zeit, Jerusalem, Ramallah, Nablus, Eyun al-Haramiya, Deir Ibzi', Deir Dibwan, Ein Qiniya, Ein 'Arik, Ladjun, Shefa'amer, Bitunya, Sattaf, Lebban, Bir Naballah, Beit Iksa, Yabroud.

Many were off-limits, inaccessible, lost in gamble. Demarcation walls, military zones, Israeli settlements got there first.

Often only traces were found — or discovered. Stepping on bush-covered earth only to uncover the remains of stone; Palestinian homes. Graveyard. Stories were once told here. Now, it is the ironic intent of occupation to reduce the storytellers themselves into the myth.

At other times, we would find in place of water, a wasteland dry and infected. More than this however, we found a land torn apart and threatened, textile robes hanging in warning ever so gently upon olive branches. Signs of utility at one extreme and protection at another. Who do you need protection from? Do we need to ask? Were we witnessing memory deletions and present-tense paranoia? Despite the obvious wounds of trauma, she (the landscape) was fighting on, preserving and thinking herself a victorious bride. She is a wonder for sore eyes! Contra-dic-tions.

Every single time, returning to Jerusalem on the days we were scouting for the sacred locations, a feeling of great heaviness burdened me because here I was, back to the bustling city, with its machines and machine operators powered to make-you-forget. I longed to go back, because in spite of their exile and their scarring, there remained a trueness.

~

Deir Dibwan/Deir Diwan waters are connected to northern Galilee — it is said the spirits that ensure this water source's life continue to do so because of a promise they made thousands of years ago.

~

In Bir Naballah, the well was once believed to be haunted by animal spirits, a fox, specifically, feared for taking the villagers' children. We find the well in the centre of the town; it is completely sealed off in concrete. Children use the concrete surface as their playground.

In the village of Ein Qiniya there are many springs, and one is believed to cure blindness. The water in this spring is still abundant and is used by Palestinian farmers to cultivate the land. It is one of the rare living springs that is still accessible to Palestinians.

There's a landscape that's suffering
Desperately seeking our attention
And we respond by living between extremes
Neither in the past nor in the present — but between feasting and fasting.
Hunger strike.
I find a dandelion
The kind ready for the wishing
Growling

Roaring
Humming
And all the other sounds (and words to describe them)

~

Terms
Terms of the springs and the jinn that guard them
As camels disguised.
There are too many disguises to keep track of.
And the names keep changing
Words versing their myths
A man invites us for tea — or is it burnt water?
He aims at our senses

~

We learn to identify the signs of nature by sounds of her inhabitants.
A pigeon cooing signals early morning or approaching dawn,
Frogs geese buzzing bees
Each song followed us throughout and became a book-mark, reference; of equations perhaps and nothing more.

~

How are we atoned? What is relegated? Promised? Compensated?

We once let our lives be ruled by tales and their metaphors.
The playground today is monitored by armed bodies claiming defence, rather than by spirits guarding sanctities.

~

A sequence of events in the lives of the dormant.
Can you say dormant to reference water? Life? Spirit, jinn,
words?
Words that speak like magic cure or poison — to bewitch
into sleep-fullness or numbness
Words that speak like chanting mumbling cures to awaken.
Just like a kiss from the deep dark 100-year-after.

~

Infinite fingers in the breeze, tall grasses
And ripples
Infinite song of birds
And frogs and bees
And barking dogs
And the quiet tapestried stillness
Of gazelles
That follow in a row
And fox that cut across the winding.

~

It is only much later that I realize one of the deer's antlers
is broken, the second deer that treks in light hops behind

the first, following faithfully, following in memory of the wound and fearing the return of its injury.

This canvas vast
Kneaded
Baked smoked
Cut eaten
Alive
Crumbs preserved for travels to unknown places —
For fear of loss.
I learn that all human beings share two fears at birth —
Fear of falling
and fear of loud noises

~

Name-change

The wells in Nablus are numerous, and their names have been changed numerously throughout time. In one location the site of the well of the old city of Nablus has today transformed into a martyr's square commemorating Palestinians who died in clashes of the Israeli-Palestinian conflict. Such is the tragedy of war, I think to myself. The living — now dead — become heroes in the eyes of the nation and are claimed by the land (as well as the people) as a legacy of the land's identity. They are given more rights in death: knighted as a form of death-right. We once sought a cure in water, but the water cannot bring back our dead, and so we now turn to concrete tales for comfort.

We have Raja's birthday party this same night, and return to the market to take his favourite sweet, *knafeh* (sweet cheese pastry). Nearby we meet a young man, a shoe-shop owner;

learning of our search, he takes us to a hidden shop that he now uses as his storage room, opens the door, points to the ceiling's concave centre and tells us in pure conviction of its passageway to Paradise. 'Do you see this dome? It is the secret doorway to the other world.'

Eyun al-Haramiya (Springs of Thieves), so named for being famously known for thievery as it was situated along the caravanserai. It is a secret mountainous hideaway Issa leads me to. The mountain has had five secret rooms carved out of it, each room entered through a colossal gateway as though built with giants in mind.

Ein al-Lebban: Here we meet a man so obsessed with his home territory that he denies anyone access — gating himself and his house, wife, and children inside. The water spring is abundant — literally gushing forth — delicious, sweet liquid blessing called water. The site of his home is an archaeological site (Khan Illiban), thus explaining his tight control. Issa and I take a liking to this dark soul and mutually agree that if we were casting for a movie in which we were looking for someone to play the part of the ghoul, this man would unquestionably get the part.

He has caged himself inside his own paradise, denying the share of wealth of the place. His overprotection of his diamond home has made him go blind.

~

Entering Beit Iksa checkpoint from Biddu village during Friday morning prayers, we meet a man standing with the young patrolling soldier. We are in search of Bir esh-Shami, a spring once believed to have been inhabited by bad spirits taking the form of any black animal. He investigates our car: 'A rental?' 'Yes.' The unknown man is awaiting a wedding party and he is standing at the checkpoint with the soldier in order to identify the wedding guests who have permits to enter the village between Israeli- and Palestinian-controlled land. He is eager to head into the village and to the wedding, but discovering the purpose of our quest, and taking an apparent liking to the adventure (a day full of adventures for him!), he diverts and leads us to a folk-taled spring that is now buried under a newly built mosque with a sealed-off water well at its footpath. It is semi-sealed off in fact. The echo of our voices reverberates into the hollowness of its belly. 'Do you want to go in?' he asks.

Exiting the village, I see a slow black cat sort of wandering about.

~

She stands at the centre
without much to say
much to say
two stripes — one on each breast —
cloak her nudity.
She is primitive
Hairy
Ape woman
Her right foot bends backward
And rests casually as in an experienced stunt
In the grasp of her left hand
In the grasp of her lost land.
Tip-toed totem.

~

mirror mirror on the Wall
hear my testimony
located relocated dislocated
a foot and a leg
a heart.
there are no silver platters for our fragmented existence.

~

It is told that a ghoul will appreciate the feed of human liver and lung and I am not sure why. Let us suppose that a ghoul represents that which is monstrous within us — and within us all — albeit in various degrees of monstrosity — and let us also suppose that a ghoul has multiple forms. A ghoul as a country, for example. A ghoul as in an authority feared, a ghoul as in an Occupation, feeding. And let's insist on proposing that the liver and lungs are not necessarily the literal bodily organs, but the organs or mechanics of any operational body or system. Do you think a country without his liver is like a water without her lungs?

There is a careful strategy, a brutal operation — sometimes visible and other times unseen — unfolding over the course of ages. I live to see the slow and wicked demise. Its initiation sponsored long before I came into being — the dispossession of the vital life-giving organs of my home. Will I live to see a resurrection of sorts? Will I live to tell? Will ghouls remain as ghouls, and shall we frame our lungs with metal to fracture biting teeth; outsmart scratching claw?

Alright, enough with my seamed metaphors. I have learned that the ghoul of the Wondertale presents little danger in comparison to the ghoulishness of mankind. I have learned that I dislike eating liver because I am afraid of my imagination upon its taste. Yet my refusal to taste liver does not console my imagination. In a similar vein, I have made several attempts at not breathing, or at holding my breath (above the water). Those familiar with my performance experiment *Holding my Breath* know. I have been obeying the order 'not a breath out of you' for far too long. It's time to reclaim lungs. Lungs, I reclaim thee. It is time to say to the water, 'Disobey.'

Disobey.

mirror mirror standing tall
tell me a story
a story do tell
comfort my spirit with the spirit of your word-memories

There was once a man who was married to a certain woman in the village of Demashq. The wife died, leaving behind a son and a daughter. One day the man married again. His new wife gave birth to two children. She fed her children only the best food, and the others she fed nothing.

The orphans would go play in the countryside and one day they found a cow, and she was not any old cow, but a magic cow! They would say to her, 'Open, O our cow!' The cow would open the space between her horns, meat and rice would come out of it, and the children would eat their fill.

When the children played together in the evening, the stepmother noticed the orphans were like red apples and thought it was peculiar since after all she was feeding them nothing. She asked her son to spy on them: 'Follow them out to the countryside and find out what they eat!'

He saw them with the cow, he heard them say, 'Open, O cow! We want to eat', and he saw what the cow could do, and he told his mother.

She made herself ill and convinced her husband that no prescription would cure her, except if he slaughtered the orphans' cow.

So he caught the cow and sacrificed her, and they ate her, while the orphans cried and cried. They were so angry that they ran away.

After some time, they reached two springs, and the boy was the first to rush and drink from the upper one. He immediately turned into a gazelle. You see, a gazelle has pissed in this spring, and whoever drinks from it turns into a gazelle.

The girl cried and cried for her brother but there was nothing they could do…

She walked until she reached the next town of Fida.

Her brother, the gazelle, always one step behind her.

They arrived by the walls of a palace and sat down. The king saw the girl — she was so beautiful — and next thing you know, they were married; and the gazelle her brother always one step behind her.

Soon it was time for the king to go to the hajj, but before leaving he said to the housekeepers, 'Take good care of my beautiful wife.'

But after he left, the housekeepers dropped the girl into a well. They fed the gazelle a mouthful of bread; they wanted to fatten him up so they could slaughter and eat him, but the gazelle would take the piece of bread they gave him and drop it into the well.

The king returned from the hajj and asked about his wife; they told him she had died and that they had buried her right under the palace floor.

The king thought something was strange, especially when he saw the gazelle disappearing into the countryside with a piece of bread in his jaws. The king followed the gazelle in order to find out where he took this food [...] and what do you think he discovered?! He saw the gazelle go to the mouth of a well, drop the bread in, and cry out:

> 'O sister O Bdur
> For me they've sharpened the knives
> And raised the pots over the fire.'

And she answered:

> 'O my little brother, O Qdur
> My hair's so long it covers me,
> In my lap sits the son of the king,
> And the whale has swallowed me.'

The king went down into the well and brought her and her child up. Then she told the king what had taken place. He took her brother and made him drink from the same spring again, and the gazelle turned back into the boy. For you see, the very spring waters that poisoned you will also set you free.

And what of the wicked housekeepers? The king had them imprisoned within the town's isolated grounds.

This is my tale. I've told it, and in your hands, I leave it.

> How many times have I told you this tale?
> Do you remember?
> We've been here before, hunting
> I felt you present and waited
>
> We were in Bir Nabala (the well of the tooth of God)
> Perfume of Za'tar
> All around us
> And as far as I can see
> And we spoke of Ma'ruf (the known)
> al-hattab (the wood-cutter)
> who spends his every day confronting ghouls (giants)

Once, just last Tuesday, in a land where thievery and barbarism were allowed, with no law against practicing either, a land where forgetfulness, too, was welcomed, there came, into the village of 'heal yourself', a man searching for a wife. Now this man's name is Ma'ruf. Soon after he entered the village, he came upon a young virgin whose name is Almaza, standing by the well across from El-Ein supermarket. Almaza was weeping and weeping her tears down the well. 'What is it that makes you cry?' he asked her. 'I weep for my lost brothers and cousins.' Ma'ruf soon learned that the village ghoul had imprisoned Almaza's brothers and cousins. Vowing to save them, Ma'ruf jumped into the well, and found the ghoul in his dwelling, sucking meat off bones.

'I will devour you next!' exclaimed the hungry ghoul.

'First, let me give you a gift I have brought you.'

'Alright then, give me your gift and I will devour you after.'

'First, tell me, what are these treasures of magic you have here on your shelf?'

'This wooden bowl — whatever you tell it to fill with — for example: "wooden bowl, fill up with rice and meat" — it will fill, and you can eat until you can barely move! This stick — if you say to it: "O my stick, keep moving, on the side of my neighbour hitting!" The stick will keep on bashing your neighbours until they return your things.'

'And these that sparkle, what are they?' asked Ma'ruf

'They are the eyes of brothers, kept in a jar. And they are the souls of cousins, kept in that jar.'

'This jar stands alone, is it the same?'

'In this jar, I keep my own soul', replied the ghoul.

Taking the jar, Ma'ruf threw it on the ground and smashed it with the magic stick until all eyes and souls were returned to their rightful bodies, and all bodies were returned to their rightful homes.

With one last blow, Ma'ruf hit the ghoul (once), and the ghoul was dead.

Ma'ruf returned to Almaza and they married. All her brothers and cousins attended the large wedding festival lavished with love, compassion, and so much food! I should know because I was there!

Now my tale does not end here for you see, at Ma'ruf and Almaza's wedding, I met a lady whose hands were made of porcelain — well no, they were not made of porcelain, but they certainly looked as though they could be. I saw her dancing, moving her hands in precious gestures like this *(show audience)*.

And her story, she told me, was that once —

Her father, broken-hearted from the death of his true love, passed away, leaving his daughter (the woman with porcelain-like hands) and her younger brother all alone.

They were children but they were strong and wise.

They had a hen that laid an egg every day, and every day they would eat the egg for breakfast and were content with their blessings. One day, when the hen strangely stopped laying eggs, the girl went to check the coop and (behold!) she discovered the place where her father (God rest his soul) had hidden all his treasure.

She did not tell her brother about the money, but she asked him: 'If someone were to show you money saved by your mother and father, what would you do with it?'

'I'd buy sheep and cattle', he answered.

His answer made her realize that he was still too young. Time passed, and she asked again, 'If someone were to show you money saved by your mother and father, what would you do with it?'

'I'd get married', he answered.

Pleased with his answer, she told him the story of the money she found, and they went searching in this world to find a bride.

Before long, they found a girl living all by herself, and he married her. She gave birth first to a girl. In the middle of the night, the woman got up, devoured her daughter, and smeared the lips of her sleeping sister-in-law with blood. When they woke up in the morning, she said to her husband, 'Your sister's a ghouleh, and she has eaten our daughter. Come take a look at her lips.'

He went and asked his sister, 'Why did you eat the girl?'

'But I didn't eat her', she answered.

The following year, after his wife gave birth to a boy, she got up in the middle of the night and ate him, again smearing her sister-in-law's lips with blood. Believing his wife, the boy was convinced he had to kill his monster-sister.

So, he took his sister to the countryside for a walk, and, after travelling a great distance, he sat her down under a tree by a well, drew his axe, and cut off her hands and her feet. As she cried, she put a curse on him: 'Brother, may a thorn get stuck in your foot, a thorn that no one can pull out and may you roam the desert for forty years.'

> Shama (the illuminated one)
> Shama was with us (here, the audience sees an image of
>   the white horse named Shama in the field)
> Dancing to
> Dogs
> Barking their bullets
> Point blank pointing
> Ring around the moon ring around the moon
> White sheep black sheep black sheep white

(return to tale)

Maybe you are wondering: what happened to the brother? Leaving his sister by the well and returning home, he witnessed his wife chase after the rooster, catch him, and devour him whole. Seeing the truth before his eyes, he realized his wife was the monster all along, not his sister. The betrayal was unbearable, and he ran away (a self-imposed exile).

After six decades of roaming, he decided to return to his hometown of Al 'Arab. It was spring, and the almond trees were blossoming.

For years he had been looking for someone to pull the thorn from his foot, though without success. Then one day, by chance, he came to his sister's doorstep. However, he did not realize that it was his sister's house.

She asked her limping brother, 'What's your problem, uncle?'

'There's a thorn in my foot', he answered, 'and nobody's been able to pull it out.'

'Come here and let me see', she said, and the thorn jumped over there. Rising to his feet, he kissed her hands.

She invited him to stay and have dinner with them.

He sat down to eat, and the children said again and again, 'Mother, tell us the story of the man who cut off the hands and feet of his sister. Did a thorn get stuck in his foot? Did he become a lion?'

The mother began to tell the tale, and at the end she told them, 'I'm the one whose hands and feet were cut off, and this man here is your uncle.'

They all got up and hugged each other. The bird has flown, and a good night to all!

> You were born of loneliness, desertedness, darkness, cracks, caves, canals, trees
> Near Al-Lozeh *(almond tree)* where you used to live
> I find Almaza *(diamond)*
> Weeping her tears
> Down the well
> Of Bir Abu Sarris *(well of the father of the thorny bush)*
> You wore a woven crimson gown
>
> Haunted by devils
> She was weeping and mourning
> 'This whole body is haunted by devils!'
> *x2*
> This limb dances in the breeze
> This one drives away the pain
> Despite every curse you throw at my face
> I still remain
>
> And no amount of trespassing will invade this gentle heart
> Inhabited or occupied or possessed
> Despite every curse you throw at my face
> I still remain
>
> How many times have I told you this tale,
> do you remember?
> In Sataf, a spirit of a man with fiery red eyes, turned to me to say,
> I am the dead forest
>
> I hear nothing under the branches of your trees
> The songs are kept for your roots only
> In a place without shadows
> They silenced my song of water
>
> Between Al-Zaitounah and Bir Zeit *(the olive and the well of oil)*
> The earth could not hold us as we moved,
>
> Falling, I heard a voice say:
> 'Do not be afraid my child; soon you will be again in your father's house.'

Of Goats and Bombs
How to Live (and Die) in an Explosive Landscape
MUNIRA KHAYYAT

INTRODUCTION

The southern borderland of Lebanon is a fertile landscape whose dwellers make a living from the land: farming tobacco for the Lebanese state-owned tobacco monopoly the Regie Libanaise de Tabacs et Tombacs, cultivating olives, keeping goats, and depending on subsistence agriculture for their daily fare.[1] This bucolic borderland is also a seasoned battlefield. Since 1948, inhabitants of the frontline villages of South Lebanon have been weathering seasons of war. Like the seasons, war is a part of life here. In South Lebanon life and war are inextricably entangled.

---

1   Many families are also partially dependent on remittances sent by relatives from abroad, but in terms of everyday livelihood they depend on the land.

This chapter explores the resistant ecology of goat herding that practically assembles life-making processes and enduring technologies of death in an artful and resistant pas de deux that is nevertheless not infallible. In what follows, I ethnographically explore the double-edged dimensions of living in militarized worlds where those who must carry on do so amidst recurrent war storms and the 'slow violence'[2] of war's enduring material remains.[3] What I call 'resistant ecologies'[4] are vitalizing practices that 'become with' the dangers inherent to a lifeworld of war.[5] They are the more-than-human relations that bind humans, animals, plants, minerals, and spirits into hardy and durable 'survival collectives' that persist across and through seasons of conflict, underwriting life, survival.[6] Through these resistant ecologies, tangles of practice that compose a dwelt landscape,[7] I elucidate an affective understanding of life in war that does not exclusively attend to war's tragic dimensions, but also actively recognizes acts of living that

2   Rob Nixon, *Slow Violence and the Environmentalism of the Poor* (Cambridge, MA: Harvard University Press, 2013).

3   Yael Navaro-Yashin, 'Affective Spaces, Melancholic Objects: Ruination and the Production of Anthropological Knowledge', *Journal of the Royal Anthropological Institute*, 15. 1 (March 2009), pp. 1–18; David Henig, 'Iron in the Soil: Living with Military Waste in Bosnia-Herzegovina', *Anthropology Today*, 28.1 (February 2012), pp. 21–23; Eleana J. Kim, 'Toward an Anthropology of Landmines: Rogue Infrastructure and Military Waste in the Korean DMZ', *Cultural Anthropology*, 31.2 (2016), pp. 162–87 <https://doi.org/10.14506/ca31.2.02>.

4   Munira Khayyat, *A Landscape of War: Ecologies of Resistance and Survival in South Lebanon* (Oakland: University of California Press, 2022).

5   Donna J. Haraway, *Staying with the Trouble: Making Kin in the Chthulucene*, Experimental Futures: Technological Lives, Scientific Arts, Anthropological Voices (Durham, NC: Duke University Press, 2016).

6   Anna Lowenhaupt Tsing, *The Mushroom at the End of the World: On the Possibility of Life in Capitalist Ruins* (Princeton, NJ: Princeton University Press, 2015).

7   Tim Ingold, 'The Temporality of the Landscape', *World Archaeology*, 25.2 (October 1993), pp. 152–74.

persist and resist amidst the debris and destruction of war. In this way, war can be recognized alongside other ruins of industrial modernity where beings strive to creatively and stubbornly hold on to life amid the wreckage.

Before war became seasonal to South Lebanon, inhabitants of Jabal 'Amil and Galilee relied on various kinds of livestock: camels, mules, donkeys, horses, cows, and goats. The use of transport and pack animals declined with the fixing of borders and the rise of motorized transport; and since the advent of war in the area, cattle have become an investment liability (too expensive to buy and feed and difficult to protect in times of active war), yet goats have continued to thrive. Goat herding continues to be practised across the borderland, and goats remain the most viable livestock in this volatile and explosive warzone because of their compatibility with wartime environments and ordnance: they are flexible and movable and can survive periods of scarcity during active war, occupations, or invasions by foraging for food and eating almost anything. And most crucially, goats are small and light and can graze in the borderland's many minefields without setting off the hidden explosives that are designed to kill humans, who are not as light-footed. This is well known among locals who send their goats to gone-wild, delicious, and deadly mined pastures. This is how an enduring, explosive military technology is both domesticated and resisted by a homegrown, anti-mine survival assemblage.

Being hardy, light, relatively inexpensive, reproducible, replaceable, and movable have enabled goats to flourish in this landscape of war. Humans have aligned their lifeways with the resistant features of these clever beasts and together these more-than-human assemblages find a way to inhabit the explosive landscape. Technologies of death are resisted by the lively multi-species ecologies of the bor-

derland but making-live by tricking mines is by no means
an easy art or an accurate science, and the threat of danger
and death remains (Figure 1). Goatherds are frequently
'kidnapped' by the Israeli army on border patrol and taken
in for questioning; their flocks are confiscated; they are
regularly accused of covering for guerrillas; they are also
often shot at if they wander too close to the border fence.
One goatherd put it to me thus: 'Because of the places we
frequent, we are distrusted by everyone.' It's a hard life, but
a life nonetheless.

THE LANDSCAPE AS WEAPON

During the 2006 'July War' between Israel and Lebanon,
and especially right as it came to a close with both sides
claiming victory,[8] Israel rained on South Lebanon —
villages, towns, roads, valleys, fields, orchards, gardens,
homes — 4.6 million cluster bombs, seeding the landscape with deadly explosives.[9] Many of the submunitions
came from expired stocks inherited by Israel from the Vietnam War, a large number of which failed to explode upon
impact, remaining in the earth as 'a deadly legacy of unexploded duds that continue to kill and injure civilians on

8   The jury is still out on which side 'won' this war but in the wake of
     the scathing report of the Winograd Commission, Israel is seen as the
     greater bungler. Hizbullah is being studied in military circles as an in-
     novative and effective fighting force (Andrew Exum, *Hizballah at War:
     A Military Assessment* (Washington, DC: Washington Institute for Near
     East Policy, 2006)), and since 2006 they have regrouped, re-armed, and
     re-entrenched themselves in their South Lebanon battlefield. In 2008
     Ehud Barak, the Israeli defence minister who replaced the disgraced
     Amir Peretz, stated that the conflict did not achieve its aim of disarming
     Hizbullah.
9   Cluster bombs were first developed during World War II. They are
     dropped in a large canister from a plane, spraying a large area with
     submunitions, or 'bomblets', with the designated intention of impeding
     an advancing army.

Figure 1. Tractor with pilfered 'Danger Mines' sign. Author's photo.

a daily basis and impede efforts to rebuild lives and live-lihoods in the wake of conflict'.[10] TeKimiti Gilbert, head of the UN Mine Action and Coordination Center (UN-MACC), whom I met in 2009 at the UNIFIL headquarters

---

10   Human Rights Watch, 'Flooding South Lebanon: Israel's Use of Cluster
      Munitions in Lebanon in July and August 2006', 16 February 2008 <https:
      //www.hrw.org/report/2008/02/16/flooding-south-lebanon/
      israels-use-cluster-munitions-lebanon-july-and-august-2006>.

in Naqura, a highly fortified barracks surrounded by blast walls and metal watchtowers, said to me:

> If you listen to the Israelis they will tell you they were targeting Hizbullah sites and Hizbullah positions. That is what they tell us is the reasoning behind where they strike. However, if you look at the ground there are a lot of areas that you can tell there were no Hizbullah positions there.
>
> To be fair there were a lot of rockets, *katyushas* being fired from orchards although I don't think that explains everything. Obviously, there was a balance; yes the Israelis were targeting Hizbullah sites, however the cluster bombs came in the last three days. So up until then there was a lot of fighting, a lot of bombs, a lot of naval gunfire, a lot of ground fire, ground fighting especially in Maroun al Ras and Bint Jbeil. But up until then, there was very limited use of cluster bombs. But in the last few days there was a curfew imposed by the Israelis saying that anyone out on the streets is a target so stay in your homes, don't move — and so people weren't moving anywhere. And the cluster bombs came in the last few days. Given the contamination we experienced after that I find it very unlikely that these cluster bombs were targeting only Hizbullah. My personal opinion is that there were three days left, the Security Council agreed on August 4th, 8 pm local time fighting stops. So both sides were taking the opportunity to inflict as much damage and destruction as they could before the ceasefire.
>
> I think the Israelis held off using cluster bombs until the end because they weren't sure whether they were going to have their own forces moving into these areas. However, once the ceasefire had been agreed to they knew that things are going to stop. So they knew that okay, three days to go. Let's just saturate the country with cluster bombs. They pointed their guns in the direction of Lebanon and then — fire!

In the words of an Israeli soldier who headed a rocket unit posted in Lebanon during the war: 'What we did was insane and monstrous, we covered entire towns in cluster bombs.'[11] Israel's 'excessive' cluster bombing of South Lebanon did 'not appear to have had any significant impact toward the military aims stated by Israel during the war. The massive and widespread use of cluster munitions across South Lebanon doesn't seem to accord with any recognizable military strategy.'[12] The head of the Danish demining outfit (DCA), who described Israel's use of cluster munitions as 'excessive', told me: 'There is no strategic pattern to cluster contamination. It is pure contamination, pure obstruction of land. When you block the land, you block the farmer's livelihood.' A former military man, the Danish deminer insisted that this cluster bombing of the landscape was excessive of military purposes. 'It is pure terror what they have done, the resistance [Hizbullah] was not in such huge areas. It is pure terror to block access to the land that is so important. A farmer's plantation or orchard is not a battle tank! *Everything* is contaminated.'[13]

No, an orchard is not a battle tank, but the ability of the southern farmer to continue to exist in this enduring battlefield is a critical dimension of the resistant nature of life across seasons of conflict in South Lebanon. By flooding the landscape with explosives, Israel sought to

---

11   Meron Rappaport, 'IDF Commander: We Fired More Than a Million Cluster Bombs in Lebanon', *Haaretz*, 12 September 2006 <https://www.haaretz.com/1.4865651> [accessed 12 November 2022].

12   Thomas Nash, *Foreseeable Harm: The Use and Impact of Cluster Munitions in Lebanon; 2006* (London: Landmine Action, 2006).

13   After the July War, an international movement against such weapons gained steam and a global treaty banning cluster munitions came into force in 2010 requiring signatories to stop the use, production, stockpiling, and transfer of the weapons. More than one hundred parties signed on, but Israel, China, the US, and Russia did not: they manufacture, sell, and stockpile most of the world's cluster munitions.

transform the living environment into a deadly weapon.[14]
By the logic of environmental warfare, Israel targeted the
landscape to disrupt the living ecologies it sustains and
contains. This 'flooding' or 'seeding' of southern land with
bombs accords with a strategy that has more to do with dis-
rupting the resistant ecologies of living across the southern
borderland. In the immediate aftermath of the war, more
than forty people were killed and nearly three hundred
were injured by land mines and unexploded cluster bombs.
A dark affective cloud clung to the landscape, the source of
life and now a place of death and danger.[15] Shortly after the
war, a humanitarian campaign was launched to clear away
the cluster bombs and about two hundred thousand were
removed, but since then the clearing effort has petered out
due to lack of funding because humanitarian relief has a
short attention span.[16] As Gilbert said to me:

> We know there are around a thousand minefields
> along the Blue Line, which equates to around
> 357,000 mines along the Blue Line, based on
> records. So the situation we have now is that there

---

14   Peter Sloterdijk, *Terror from the Air*, trans. by Amy Patton and Steve
      Corcoran, Semiotext(e) Foreign Agents Series (Los Angeles: Semio-
      text(e); distributed by MIT Press, 2009); Ian G. R. Shaw, 'Scorched
      Atmospheres: The Violent Geographies of the Vietnam War and the
      Rise of Drone Warfare', *Annals of the American Association of Geograph-
      ers*, 106.3 (2016), pp. 688–704 <https://doi.org/10.1080/00045608.
      2015.1115333>; Chris Pearson, 'Researching Militarized Landscapes:
      A Literature Review on War and the Militarization of the Environ-
      ment', *Landscape Research*, 37.1 (2012), pp. 115–33 <https://doi.org/
      10.1080/01426397.2011.570974>.

15   Munira Khayyat and Rabih Shibli, 'Tobacco Olives and Bombs: Recon-
      figuration and Recovery of Landscape in Postwar Southern Lebanon',
      in *The Right to Landscape: Contesting Landscape and Human Rights*, ed.
      by Shelley Egoz, Jala Makhzoumi, and Gloria Pungetti (Farnham, UK:
      Ashgate, 2012), pp. 263–76.

16   Didier Fassin, *Humanitarian Reason: A Moral History of the Present
      Times* (Berkeley: University of California Press, 2012).

are still cluster bombs in the South and there's a
lot less than when we first started back in 2006,
and it's been almost three years now of clearance
and there's been a lot of clearance conducted, a
lot of money has gone into this. Around 190,000
cluster bombs that we know about that have been
located and destroyed, which is a joint effort from
the Lebanese Army, the UNIFIL teams and the
civilian organizations that we have working here.
The job isn't finished, there's still work to be done.
But like everything else, Lebanon is now falling
off the world's attention. Until the next conflict,
whenever it happens. And that's the reality. The
international community loses interest. In 2007,
at the height of mine clearance activity, we had 61
cluster teams, in 2008 they dropped to 44, and in
2009 at the start of this year, we started with 40
and we've now dropped down to around 27 teams
now, so it's a third of the team we had back in 2007.

More than one million cluster bombs, not counting landmines, remain in the earth of South Lebanon. According to
the mines expert, relatively speaking and despite its 'post-
age stamp' size, Lebanon is the country worst affected by
cluster bombs worldwide in terms of contamination density. Cluster bombs and mines as physical remnants of war
become entangled with the lives and livelihoods of the
borderland's inhabitants even in periods when wartime violence is not acute. Dwellers of the southern borderland
must contend with the deadly nature of the land to continue to live there. This is where dangers arise. Gilbert
stressed that mines and cluster bombs become a problem
when people use the land:

> Up until May 2000 the mines weren't a really
> big problem. Because [of the Israeli occupation]
> people weren't using the land extensively. Rela-
> tively speaking there was less agriculture going
> on … However, after the withdrawal, as you can

imagine, there was a lot of happiness and people
came flooding back to the South and they were
confronted by these minefields. And there were a
lot of accidents that occurred just after the withdrawal because people were unaware of the mines
and people were desperate to cultivate the land
and get their livelihoods restarted again. [Because
of the enduring war condition] the Lebanese government excluded a number of areas [from mine
clearance]: the Blue Line and minefields north of
the Litani River. The people who are suffering are
the villages on the Blue Line [the borderland vil-
lages] because during the occupation they were
denied their land. The Israelis left nine years ago
now and nine years later, they are still in the same
situation as when the Israelis were occupying the
South. The villagers can't use their land and land is
valuable in the South and not only for agriculture
but also for grazing. So every meter of land for
them is of use and value. If we could clear that
land of minefields and release the land back to the
people it would be so much better for them.

As Brennon Jones, the author of a *New York Times* article
entitled 'Southern Lebanon's Deadly Crop' writes:

Deny farmers their land and they'll risk life and
limb. It's the same in southern Lebanon today as
it was in South Vietnam in the early 1970s. In Vietnam, where I was a journalist and social worker in
the early 1970s, I saw farmers forced off their land
by American and South Vietnamese bombing and
corralled into refugee camps to keep them from returning. […] But many of these rural Vietnamese
[…] were desperate to return to their land and to
farming, the only livelihood they had ever known.
They broke out of the barbed-wire encampments
and rushed for home, only to be maimed and
killed by the cluster bomblets that littered their
land.

> History is now repeating itself in the cruellest ways in southern Lebanon. It's the farmers once again who are bearing the greatest physical and economic toll from unexploded cluster bomb sub-munitions. An estimated one million such bomblets now contaminate the farmland and residential areas of southern Lebanon — a deadly calling card left by Israeli forces as they departed Lebanon at the end of this year's 34-day war.[17]

The villagers across the farming villages of the southern borderland who have been living through wars for generations now and do not have many alternatives to fall back on are literally taking matters into their own hands. They cannot passively accept the lethal weaponization of the landscape, the major source of their livelihoods and subsistence, and although there are risks involved, they continue to pursue their livelihoods amidst militarized ecologies, 'becoming with' the deadly technologies that seek to disrupt their lifeways.

Eleana Kim's work on mines as 'rogue infrastructure' in the Korean DMZ illuminates the interaction of mines and humans who find ways of living with them. 'Mines can function effectively as area-denial weapons when their existence is discovered, most tragically after someone has been killed or injured. [...] Yet the ability of mines to deter human trespass is also viewed as a form of social control, surveillance and dispossession, which some villagers resist, especially as they will not let perfectly good land remain uncultivated.'[18] The interactive agency of explosives and humans and goats in the South Lebanon setting is productive of resistant, more-than-human ecologies and

---

17 Brennon Jones, 'Southern Lebanon's Deadly Crop', *New York Times*, 12 October 2006.

18 Kim, 'Toward an Anthropology of Landmines', pp. 177–78.

landscapes that refuse the military impositions of deadly technology aiming to enforce limits and controls on life and movement. These lively and affective ecologies shape resistant life in this explosive borderland.

DOMESTICATING BOMBS

We plunge into the deep valley enclosing freshwater springs and 'health fortifying' forests and follow the thalweg that sinks down in a green zigzag between two level plateaus facing each other on either side of sheer cliffs, north and south. The valley transforms into a defensive trench during times of conflict as it gashes across the north-south trajectory of offensive and defensive warfare: shallow and wide along the coast in the west, it narrows as it cuts east and then widens again as it approaches a village nestled in a crook at the head of the rift, but the plains on either side increase in elevation as they march away from the coast. During the occupation, this valley formed a part of the northern border of the occupation zone. Thus, for twenty-two years it was rife with resistance activity (surveillance, reconnaissance, and infiltration), UNIFIL activity (observation and obstruction), and Israeli offensive bombardment. Due to its geography and location, this leafy valley was off-limits to villagers and a place of wilderness and war. Since the occupation ended in 2000, villagers have reclaimed parts of it, especially where the freshwater spring bubbles out of the earth, even venturing farther into the woodland. But after the 2006 war, the valley once again became a place of danger and death as the Israeli air force peppered it with cluster bombs to discourage villagers as much as guerrillas from frequenting it. Still, inhabitants of the surrounding villages will not be thwarted. Families picnic, swim, and wash in the stream, and some — out of necessity — venture even farther, taking the valley's explosive nature in stride.

Following a dusty dirt track leading past a chalk quarry on our left, we soon come upon villagers cooling off by the rock pools to our right. Families with small children sit and play in and around the green water. We continue along the dirt path, cleaving to a passage on a ledge against the sheer northern face of the valley wall, plunging deeper into the undergrowth crowding upon us in a friendly, pushy way from either side. Soon we realize that we have stumbled across a network of foxholes, bunkers, and dugouts — active or defunct? Not clear, but most likely the latter. The ones we recognize seem to be in a state of disrepair — hence we recognize them! Plastic pipes stick out in odd places from under the earth. Under canopies of bouncy greenery, wooden planks reinforce a foxhole entrance and discarded pieces of olive-coloured ammunition boxes are strewn here and there. Soon the path ends in a pile of rocks across the way, and the undergrowth surges beyond us, indicating the way forward — but not for us. A rash of poisonous pink oleander brightens the forested foot of the valley, following where the water runs and where we can only go with our eyes. We look up toward the lip of the gorge and the sky and note along the way several black cave mouths silenced with twigs and branches like fingers lifted to mouths: *shhhhh*. We silently turn back.

This valley is the everyday haunt of goatherds and their flocks of nimble goats. Beginning at the entrance of the valley at dawn, the goats and their human companions, *israh*, wander slowly up the valley along the water source, spreading out to browse and graze along the flanks of the valley as it deepens. Goats and goatherd 'heft'[19] to the hills with

---

19   John Gray, 'Open Spaces and Dwelling Places: Being at Home on Hill Farms in the Scottish Borders', *American Ethnologist*, 26.2 (May 1999), pp. 440–60.

a 'centaurian synergy of human and beast' and together encounter the war objects nestled in the geography.[20] The valley is an ideal grazing ground: due to heightened military presence and sensitivity it is uncultivated, wild and overgrown. And since it is not private property, the grazing of the goats can proceed without trespass.

At the head of the valley path, in the clearing by the rock pools, we meet Abu Bilal, a Bedouin goatherd, with his goats. Sun-wizened, spare, and wiry, and bent at the hip in a perpetual upward gait, he resembles the goats he spends his days with. A bit of twine pokes out between the buttons of his grubby shirt and he holds a black nylon bundle in the crook of his arm: lunch. Every morning, as the sun makes its way up the antemeridian sky, he makes his way up the valley from a village toward the west with his twenty goats and ten cows. The cows he leaves near the water in the lower levels of the valley to cool off as the day warms, and he continues along the steep flanks of the borderland hills with his sprightly and nimble goats. Inhabiting these hillsides for all of his life, Abu Bilal has an intuitive sense and practised knowledge of its characteristics, features, flora, and fauna. This is why he does not fear the potentially dangerous landscape he treks through with his goat companions, as long as the sun is in the sky. He knows the landscape well: the wild pigs stay in the foot of the valley and emerge only at night. The hyenas remain high up in the craggy peaks and if one approaches, the goatherd tells us he holds a rock high over his head and shows no fear until the hyena backs off.

---

20 Tim Ingold and Jo Lee Vergunst, 'Introduction', in *Ways of Walking: Ethnography and Practice on Foot*, ed. by Tim Ingold and Jo Lee Vergunst (London: Routledge, 2008), pp. 1–20 (p. 12).

> We 'Arab, we Bedu are history and geography be-
> cause we have been living for generations in this
> land. And the son of the wilderness, *barr*, doesn't
> fear, he stays brave. He walks in the night and he
> walks in the day and he doesn't fear. I walk in the
> night and my step is sure. I submit to nobody ex-
> cept God who created me. The brave man is not
> shaken, not by wind and not by a mountain. I am
> *bajiss*, courageous! I don't fear the wilderness or
> anything in it — except perhaps those.

He points, and sure enough, at his feet near a pink oleander *difla* is a small, perfectly spherical cluster bomb (Figure 2). The bomb has been surrounded by rocks and marked with blue spray paint by demining crews. Abu Bilal the goatherd says that he is constantly on the lookout for bomblets while wandering with his goats. 'They are all over the *wa'r* [wilderness]. When I find a bomb, I surround it with rocks and cover it with a bigger rock so that I don't trip on it' — he crouches down close to the small, spherical bomb to demonstrate and I instinctively take a step back. Straightening up, he continues, 'I try to remember the location of the bombs I have encountered to avoid stepping on them as I walk.' Abu Bilal's method is surely not infallible, but it does not hinder him from venturing forth. For one who intimately and deeply inhabits this geography and who makes a living, and a landscape, by traveling through it, the bombs — and other war-related objects, structures, beings, networks — must be managed. As a long-term dimension of war, explosives in the landscape shape an affective ecology that must be inhabited by some. Bombs entangle with the lifeways of goats and humans in this warzone, making a difficult life even more precarious, and yet they do not entirely hinder the pursuit of life and livelihoods as resistant, multispecies assemblages find ways to co-exist with them.

Figure 2. Abu Bilal points to a cluster bomb. Author's photo.

Because the uncultivated land is low priority in terms of demining, there is little chance that it will ever be cleared, and the cluster bombs remain hidden there year after year as volatile, explosive secrets in the undergrowth and soil. In the meantime, Abu Bilal has little choice but to continue to make a living; his and his goats' affective relationship to this valley tempers somewhat the danger of the bombs, and so feet and hooves continue on their daily pathways as they walk together through the warscape (Figure 3). 'With such a close, centaurian synergy of human and beast, it is difficult to assign agency unequivocally to one side or the other. […] [Pastoralists become in effect] human-animal hybrids whose combined feet and hooves move in unison and whose perception is attuned to features of the world of common concern to such compound beings', write Tim Ingold and Jo Lee Vergunst.[21] This multi-species hybrid incorporates the presence of the bombs into their intimate, practised knowledge of the landscape. By navigating bombs, they domesticate them as a part of their habitat. Bombs become features of this 'centaurian' lifeworld. Bombs have been drawn into the realm of the ordinary object goats and goatherds encounter and navigate, like poisonous plants, hyenas, and wild pigs. They are as constitutive of their geographies, their everyday worlds.

One of the primary reasons that goats thrive in the minefields of the South Lebanon warscape is that they are too light to spring mines. Back at his office, Gilbert showed me a mine and explained how it works — most interestingly, how it works against humans (and cows) but not against goats:

> Gilbert: I will show you an example of a mine here. This is a number 4 anti-personnel mine, Israeli-made. That's all it is: a plastic casing. This used to be a live mine but the explosives have been taken out — two hundred grams of explosives connected with a fuse. As you can see here it has a lid, a collar. The collar sits on the firing pin and it is laid under the ground like this, around two to three inches below the surface and the pressure of a person standing on that pushes the lid down

---

21   Ingold and Vergunst, 'Introduction', p. 12.

Figure 3. Goats and goatherd walk alongside the mined
border. Author's photo.

which pushes the collar away which lets the firing
pin go forward and it explodes — and it all happens within a flash. A millisecond.

Me: It's so small, huh?

Gilbert: Yeah, but it is powerful. Two hundred
grams of explosives is enough to take your leg off.
But because goats are relatively light compared
to a person, these things can often take five to
seven kilograms of weight but that depends on the
depth of the mine, how deep it has been laid. So

generally, goats are not heavy enough to set off one of these mines and the farmers know this. And they also know that the good grazing land is inside the minefield fencing. The grass there is a lot better and so they let the goats go inside and then, taking the risk that, you know, these goats aren't heavy enough. However, every now and then cows get inside and cows set things off. So, we had a number of accidents with cows losing their legs and then they're sitting in the minefield and the farmer goes into the minefield to get the cow and gets killed.

The practice of herding is a key landscape practice tying people to place and one that becomes more difficult as commons are privatized and national borders harden.[22] In the case of South Lebanon, the limits on movement are not so much due to the enclosing and delimiting of private property but instead to the lethal presence of unexploded mines and cluster bombs, especially in the pasturelands along the Lebanese–Israeli border and frontline. But Abu Bilal and his goats adapted their pastoral pathways to encompass those deadly remnants in the land. Abu Bilal continues walking with his goats and underfoot, a landscape and lifeworld resistantly unfolds. Their path has not yet been interrupted by bombs (or other war-related difficulties); for Abu Bilal and his goats these are navigable. He is fearless, *bajiss*, confident in his knowledge, and with his goats his step is sure. These encounters with bombs in the landscape domesticate them, tame them, bring them into a practised lifeworld. Goat herding along the Lebanese–Israeli border is a precarious practice, yet some are not as fortunate as Abu Bilal and his goats have been thus far.

---

22   Gray, 'Open Spaces and Dwelling Places'; Kenneth Olwig, 'Performing on the Landscape versus Doing Landscape: Perambulatory Practice, Sight and the Sense of Belonging', in *Ways of Walking*, ed. by Ingold and Vergunst, pp. 81–92.

OF MINES AND MEN[23]

It is Sunday in this small border village, the day when families, dispersed across the generations, gather. Abu Nimr sits in the courtyard of his home in the midst of many: his grown children, their spouses, and their children. He looks lost — forlorn and quite alone despite the cheerful hubbub around him. The low buildings around the central space are an eclectic mix of old and new, used and abandoned, ruined and maintained. The older structures were used as enclosures for a flock of hundreds of goats but today there is no trace of their former inhabitants apart from the empty troughs lining the sides of one wall, carved into the mud plaster. These structures are now filled with golden loops of tobacco hanging from the wooden rafters. I sat and spoke for a long time with the *tarrash*, the old goatherd, who had sold off his entire flock — the last animal just two months ago — and given up his lifelong practice after the death of his son Ali only a few years ago.

Ali was Abu Nimr's fifth child and the only one among his ten siblings who had left school and instead learned from his father (and their goats) how to walk the warscape. 'Ali had it in him', the old man says, rubbing his reddening eyes, which made the blue of the irises stand out even more brightly. 'Ali was interested in the work. The moment he learned how to walk he was walking with me with the *ma'za* goats. Ali learned to communicate with the beasts and he had the stamina to be out in the *wa'r* wilderness under the sun all day.' Ali continued to accompany his father and

---

23 Goat herding in South Lebanon is predominantly the domain of men. There is the occasional female goatherd, but I did not have the opportunity to work with them. In my forthcoming book, *A Landscape of War: Ecologies of Resistance and Survival*, I examine several ecologies, one of which, tobacco farming, is predominantly engaged in by women.

their flock of more than five hundred goats through the borderland pastures in the landscape around their village; they would often run into trouble. More than once they were shot at. The old man took a bullet in his arm and was detained for questioning by Palestinian guerrillas and then by the Israeli Army on several occasions.

Goats are nimble, intelligent, yet 'anarchistic and whimsical' beings who browse the landscape for edibles, climbing up rocks, cliffs, and even trees to grab a nibble.[24] They communicate well with their human companions, who sense their mood and work with it, communicating through a combination of sound and movement as they alternately follow and lead them through the landscape. Abu Nimr found that his goats' nervous temperament and light-footedness worked well in the militarizing milieu. Together, human and animal adapted to the military realities of their habitat. 'Goats sense danger before humans do, they would always tell me when something was not right — whether it was a snake in the bushes or Israeli infiltrators or guerrillas.' Abu Nimr continued goat herding even during the difficult years of the Palestinian guerrilla war along the border, up until the 1978 Israeli invasion. After the 1982 Israeli invasion barrelled over the hill and through their village and by the time the Israeli occupation had entrenched itself in 1985, things were relatively easier for Abu Nimr and his goats, as the lines of battle had settled farther away from their village and pastures, north of the international borderline that ran all along the southern edge of the village. 'During the occupation, there were clear limits as to where we could go and when we could be at pasture', Abu Nimr says. During

---

24   Pernille Gooch, 'Feet Following Hooves', in *Ways of Walking*, ed. by Ingold and Vergunst, pp. 67–80 (p. 70).

this time, one of his sons served as soldier in the SLA. This necessary sacrifice allowed the family some breathing room to continue to live within the occupation. As the rest of his sons neared adulthood, they left for Beirut to avoid conscription. There, one became a policeman, another a schoolteacher, and another a journalist while Abu Nimr, Ali, and the goats continued to walk the borderland. After the end of the occupation, Ali and his father continued to walk with their goats, selling kids, manure, milk. It was a decent living, bringing in, according to Abu Nimr, about twenty-five million liras a year.[25] Yet the warscape shifted once again when the Israelis suddenly withdrew from South Lebanon in May 2000. New realities came to define the geography — the border between Lebanon and Israel was once again a front slicing along the southern edge of their village.

On the day he died, Ali was walking along the main strip of road which runs parallel to and is barely twenty meters removed from the Lebanese–Israeli border. This would have been impossible during the occupation, when any movement on the main road, which was priority access for the Israeli military and their allies, was strictly circumscribed and often violently controlled. In the wake of the Israeli withdrawal, new freedoms and new restrictions emerged. There was a period of uncertainty and trial and error as people gingerly came to get a feel for this new ground, this new reality that was overwriting but not quite replacing the order of the occupation. This space of rupture, both political and physical, is where Ali died. Having inhabited the occupation order since he was six, he was familiar with its dimensions, dangers, and limits. It was in the more unfamiliar (if relatively less encumbered) period

---

25   The equivalent of sixteen thousand US dollars.

that followed that he lost his footing and stumbled upon a mine the occupiers had left behind.

As his father greyed, Ali began to take over more and more of the strenuous work. One bright cold day in November 2005, Ali was heading back home alone with the flock after a long day at pasture. The goats swarmed along the main road leading toward the village that runs adjacent to a well-known minefield. Heading east with the setting sun at his back, Ali came up behind as the goats fanned out to the left of the road where the land rose into a gentle slope. To the right, where the minefield snaked along, accompanying the goatherd and his flock, the land fell steeply into a shallow plain beyond which the technical fence defining the northern limits of Israel bluntly truncated the landscape. Suddenly, a goat lost its footing and stumbled down the short ledge to the shallow grassland that hid mines. Although there were no markings to indicate a minefield, Ali knew too well what this stretch of earth concealed and moved quickly to help the goat regain its footing. Ali's instinct for danger was correct but he acted in haste. Stepping off the asphalt to urge the goat back to the road, he stepped on the mine that the goat had probably trod on and did not trigger. In his instinctive rush to guide his goat to safety, Ali met his death. He was thirty-three years old. He left behind a wife, two young children, and an unborn child. His widow sits in a drift of green tobacco as Abu Nimr tells the story. She is dressed in black from head to toe. Her two daughters, who are now five and three, help with the work of *shakk*, threading the tobacco leaves, and the boy, who is about seven, hangs around listening to his grandfather talk (Figure 4). After Ali's early death, Abu Nimr tried to take up goat herding again, but could not manage. After falling and breaking his arm, he was urged by his wife and children to give up goat herding and soon he had no choice but to give in. His body was no longer able. Little by little he sold his flock of seven hundred, and now, after lifetimes and generations, this family's goat-herding practice has come to an end. 'I am left alone without my son, without my goats.' Although Abu Nimr continues to exist here on earth, there is something hollow, something lifeless in his demeanour and presence. In fact, the old man does look lost. He wanders over to thread some tobacco with the women and children, but he does it half-heartedly and soon drops the thread and begins to cry. His grandchildren clamber around him, accustomed (but not oblivious) to his mournful demeanour. He lights another cigarette.

None of Abu Nimr's descendants will walk with goats along the southern borders of Lebanon again. His living sons are employed and live in the cities, and apart from the eldest, who owns the village gas station, have established lives away from the village. Generally speaking, once someone leaves the village and a rural way of life, there is no turning back. Education, employment, and urban dwelling are considered a step up in life and hence few return. These days Abu Nimr spends most of his time sitting in the village square with other old men, smoking hand-chopped tobacco from their own fields. The income lost by the end of his flock is now gained by leaning more heavily on the tobacco that the women (wives of sons, granddaughters) of his household work; he sometimes helps the women and children in threading, something a young man would never consider doing. So, although years have passed since Ali was killed by a mine, this old man cannot stop crying over his death: at once the death of a son and a practiced livelihood — a lifeworld and a landscape.

Bereft of his son and his flock, Abu Nimr has nothing more to say to me today. Choked with sobs, he shuffles off to sit among his household's women and children. His

Figure 4. Abu Nimr, his grandchildren, and the widow of his
son Ali. Author's photo.

living sons — some of whom are here today — take up the
thread of the conversation when their father stops. They
have set up a shrine to their lost brother in their home.
They take me up there to have a look. As I gaze into the
photographed face of Ali, a spare young man with the fair
complexion, bony face, and light eyes of his father, I think
about how, as certain rural livelihoods become harder to
maintain, tobacco, the bright green cash crop, almost always takes their place. As people let go of long traditions

of practice in the face of insurmountable war-related obs-
tacles, tobacco is often all that remains. Tobacco, the 'bitter
crop' is a cash crop and resistant ecology continues to
underwrite the possibility of life in the South Lebanon warzone because it thrives within the conditions of poverty,
and through seasons of war.

In my work, I draw attention to war as a place of life
and to the combined agency of its human and more-than-
human dwellers in resisting this deadly condition through
ordinary acts of living. As 'amm Dawud, a frontline villa-
ger, sputtered in exasperation as I kept asking him about
the mines while he described to me in loving detail how
he cared for his beloved olive trees along the borderline:
'*ya binti, al mawt bi rizq al insan!* Daughter, death is in
human livelihood! That is simply the way it is. *Min il bahr
lal mtulleh, min hon la akher m'ammar allah.* From the sea
to Metulla! From here to the very end of God's earth!
Khalas, what can you do?' Far from illustrating a fatalism
often ascribed to peasants, the quintessential subalterns,
the 'weak',[26] such 'acceptance' of the dimensions of surviving in this place, the 'making do' of just continuing to live
here demonstrates an active form of life-making.[27] It shows
us the everyday 'art of doing',[28] the deft ability of ordinary
people on the margins of the nation-state — of history,[29]
of the social, the economic, and the political but too often
at the centre of violent action — to navigate, inhabit, and
in this way resist an always precarious, enduringly lethal

---

26   James C. Scott, *Weapons of the Weak: Everyday Forms of Peasant Resist-
     ance* (New Haven, CT: Yale University Press, 2000).

27   Michel de Certeau, *The Practice of Everyday Life*, trans. by Steven F.
     Rendall, 2nd pr. (Berkeley: University of California Press, 2013).

28   Ibid.

29   Michel-Rolph Trouillot, *Silencing the Past: Power and the Production of
     History*, 5th pr. (Boston, MA: Beacon Press, 2001).

terrain that remains the primary place and source of life and living.

POSTSCRIPT

Sometimes life is stranger than fiction. On 5 July 2017, Abu Nimr, after decades of cohabiting with technologies of death, stepped on a mine while herding his beloved goats and died. He had returned to goat herding soon after I saw him in 2009. His wife and children relented and allowed him to re-establish a smaller, more manageable herd, as they saw that he truly could not live without his goats. On the day he died, a kid had wandered away from the flock and into the minefield. Like his son before him, he followed her and in doing so stepped on a mine that the goat most likely trod on and did not spring. When I first heard the tragic news, I couldn't believe it. It was an ending that seemed almost scripted, but there was nothing fictional about this. Mines are an enduring legacy of war that continue to kill and maim, long after war is over.

This essay ends on a tragic note as a reminder of the lethal remains of war, its slow violence, its *longue durée*. Still, in my work on resistant ecologies in a landscape of war, I focus on life and its creative strategies within this militarized milieu. The daily practices of those inhabiting wars are dominated by the fight for life every day. Some may lose this war, but some win.

References

66th Military Intelligence Battalion website, last modified 26 July 2018 <https://www.inscom.army.mil/msc/66mib/24thMI.html>

Բաղբրջի, in *Tigris-Dikris Almanac* (Aleppo: Digranakerd Compatriotic and Reconstruction Union, 1946), p. 36

Açıksöz, Salih Can, *Sacrificial Limbs: Masculinity, Disability, and Political Violence in Turkey* (Berkeley: University of California Press, 2019) <https://doi.org/10.2307/j.ctvqr1b4n>

Ahıska, Meltem, 'Occidentalism and Registers of Truth: The Politics of Archives in Turkey', *New Perspectives on Turkey*, 34 (2006), pp. 9–29 <https://doi.org/10.1017/S0896634600004350>

Akarçay, Ayça, Nurhan Davutyan, and Sezgin Polat, *Economic Consequences of Demographic Engineering: Turkey and WWI* (Rochester, NY: Social Science Research Network, 15 April 2021) <https://doi.org/10.2139/ssrn.3828518>

Allen, Jafari Sinclaire, and Ryan Cecil Jobson, 'The Decolonizing Generation: (Race and) Theory in Anthropology since the Eighties', *Current Anthropology*, 57.2 (2016), 129–48 <https://doi.org/10.1086/685502>

Atılgan, Mehmet, Mehmet Polatel, Nora Mildanoğlu, and Özgür Leman Eren, eds, *2012 Beyannamesi: İstanbul Ermeni Vakıflarının El Konan Mülkleri / 2012 Declaration: The Seized Properties of Armenian Foundations in Istanbul* (Istanbul: Hrant Dink Vakfı Yayınları, 2012) <https://hrantdink.org/tr/bolis/faaliyetler/projeler/kulturel-miras/149-2012-beyannamesi-istanbul-ermeni-vakiflarinin-el-konan-mulkleri>

Başkaya, Zafer, 'Diyarbakır İli İpekböcekçiliğinin Türkiye'de Yeri ve Mekansal Analizi' [The Place and Spatial Analysis of Sericulture in Diyarbakir Province of Turkey], in *Uluslararası Diyarbakır Sempozyumu*, ed. by Ufuk Bircan, Aytaç Coşkun, Mustafa Temel, and Pınar Gürhan Kılıç (Diyarbakır: T. C. Diyarbakır Valiliği Kültür Sanat Yayınları, 2017), XVIII, pp. 2191–2217

Berg, Ulla D., and Ana Y. Ramos-Zayas, 'Racializing Affect: A Theoretical Proposition', *Current Anthropology*, 56.5 (2015), pp. 654–77 <https://doi.org/10.1086/683053>

Bessire, Lucas, and David Bond, 'Ontological Anthropology and the Deferral of Critique', *American Ethnologist*, 41.3 (2014), pp. 440–56 <https://doi.org/10.1111/amet.12083>

Biner, Zerrin Özlem, *States of Dispossession: Violence and Precarious Coexistence in Southeast Turkey* (Philadelphia: University of Pennsylvania Press, 2020) <https://doi.org/10.9783/9780812296594>

Bourriaud, Nicolas, 'Curator's Statement', *Istanbul Foundation for Culture and Arts*, 2019 <https://bienal.iksv.org/en/16th-istanbul-biennial/curator-s-statement> [accessed 30 March 2022]

Butler, Judith, *Frames of War: When Is Life Grievable?* (London: Verso, 2016)

Cadena, Marisol de la, *Earth Beings: Ecologies of Practice across Andean Worlds* (Durham, NC: Duke University Press, 2016)

Card, James, 'Paradise in No Man's Land', *Earth Island Journal*, 23.1 (Spring 2008): *The Argicultural Issue*, pp. 51–54 <https://www.earthisland.org/journal/index.php/magazine/entry/paradise_in_no_mans_land/> [accessed 22 March 2022]

Castelier, Sebastian, and Quentin Muller, 'Gravediggers Claim Ghosts Haunt World's Largest Cemetery in Iraq', *Al Jazeera*, 10 September 2019 <https://www.aljazeera.com/features/2019/9/10/gravediggers-claim-ghosts-haunt-worlds-largest-cemetery-in-iraq>

Çelik, Adnan, and Ergin Öpengin, 'The Armenian Genocide in the Kurdish Novel: Restructuring Identity through Collective Memory', *European Journal of Turkish Studies. Social Sciences on Contemporary Turkey*, 2016 <https://doi.org/10.4000/ejts.5291>

Çelik, Adnan, and Namık Kemal Dinç, *Yüz Yıllık Ah! Toplumsal Hafızanın İzinde: 1915 Diyarbekir* (İstanbul: İsmail Beşikçi Vakfı, 2015)

Çerçiyan, Yeğişe, *Nor Dikaranagerd*, 20.2 (1937), pp. 5–6

Certeau, Michel de, *The Practice of Everyday Life*, trans. by Steven F. Rendall, 2nd pr. (Berkeley: University of California Press, 2013)

Coates, Peter, 'Borderland, No-Man's Land, Nature's Wonderland', *Environment and History*, 20.4 (November 2014), pp. 499–516 <https://doi.org/10.3197/096734014X14091313617244>

Corrigan, Lisa M., *Black Feelings: Race and Affect in the Long Sixties* (Jackson: University Press of Mississippi, 2020) <https://doi.org/10.14325/mississippi/9781496827944.001.0001>

Coulthard, Glen Sean, *Red Skin, White Masks: Rejecting the Colonial Politics of Recognition* (Minneapolis: University of Minnesota Press, 2014) <https://doi.org/10.5749/minnesota/9780816679645.001.0001>

Critchley, Simon, *Infinitely Demanding: Ethics of Commitment, Politics of Resistance* (London: Verso Books, 2007)

Dewachi, Omar, *Ungovernable Life: Mandatory Medicine and Statecraft in Iraq* (Stanford, CA: Stanford University Press, 2019)

Dündar, Fuat, *İttihat Ve Terakki'nin Müslümanları İskan Politikasi (1913–1918)* (Istanbul: İletişim Yayınları, 2001)

—— *Modern Türkiye'nin Şifresi: İttihat Ve Terakki'nin Ethnisite Mühendisliği, 1913–1918* (Istanbul: İletişim Yayınları, 2008)

Duggan, Wayne, 'Best Defense Stock to Buy Now', *US News and World Report*, 8 March 2022 <https://money.usnews.com/investing/slideshows/best-defense-stocks-to-buy-now> [accessed 22 March 2022]

Ekmekçioğlu, Lerna, 'Of Dark Pasts and Pipe Dreams: The Turkish University', *YILLIK: Annual of Istanbul Studies*, 3 (2021), pp. 185–93 <https://doi.org/10.53979/yillik.2021.12>

—— *Recovering Armenia: The Limits of Belonging in Post-Genocide Turkey* (Stanford: Stanford University Press, 2016) <https://doi.org/10.1515/9780804797191>

Ellison, Sarah, and Travis M. Andrews, '"They Seem So Like Us": In Depicting Ukraine's Plight, Some in Media Use Offensive Comparisons', *The Washington Post*, 27 February 2022 <https://www.washingtonpost.com/media/2022/02/27/media-ukraine-offensive-comparisons/>

Exum, Andrew, *Hizballah at War: A Military Assessment* (Washington, DC: Washington Institute for Near East Policy, 2006)

Fassin, Didier, *Humanitarian Reason: A Moral History of the Present Times* (Berkeley: University of California Press, 2012) <https://doi.org/10.1525/9780520950481>

Fay, George R., 'Investigation of the Abu Ghraib Detention Facility and 205th Military Intelligence Brigade MG', 2004 <https://www.thetorturedatabase.org/document/fay-report-investigation-205th-military-intelligence-brigades-activites-abu-ghraib>

'Feral Atlas Collective', *Istanbul Foundation for Culture and Arts*, 2019 <https://bienal.iksv.org/en/bienal-artists/feral-atlas-collective> [accessed 30 March 2022]

Fernando, Mayanthi L., 'Supernatureculture', *The Immanent Frame*, 11 December 2017 <https://tif.ssrc.org/2017/12/11/supernatureculture/>

Fittkau, Ludger, 'Kampftraining im Naturschutzgebiet: Kriegs-übungen der US-Army im Mainzer Sand lösen Protest aus', Deutschlandradio, 31 May 2012, 14:17:31–14:23:09 (no longer online, but available upon request from Deutschlandradio Archiv)

Flintam, Matthew, 'Parallel Landscapes: A Spatial and Critical Study of Militarised Sites in the United Kingdom' (PhD diss., Royal College of Art, 2010)

Galeano, Eduardo, *The Open Veins of Latin America: Five Centuries of the Pillage of a Continent*, trans. by Cedric Belfrage (New York: Monthly Review Press, 1973)

Ghanam, Farhan, *Remaking the Modern: Space, Relocation, and the Politics of Identity in a Global Cairo* (Berkeley, CA: University of California Press, 2002) <https://doi.org/10.1525/9780520936010>

Gilmore, Ruth Wilson, 'Abolition Geography and the Problem of Innocence', in *Futures of Black Radicalism*, ed. by Gaye Theresa Johnson and Alex Lubin (London: Verso Books, 2017), pp. 225–40

—— *Abolition on Stolen Land*, online video recording of the keynote address of the public programme 'Sanctuary Spaces: Reworlding Humanism', 9 October 2020, UCLA Luskin Institute on Inequality and Democracy, Vimeo <https://vimeo.com/467484872#t=1543s> [accessed 24 March 2022].

—— *Golden Gulag: Prisons, Surplus, Crisis, and Opposition in Globalizing California* (Berkeley: University of California Press, 2006)

Gooch, Pernille, 'Feet Following Hooves', in *Ways of Walking*, ed. by Ingold and Vergunst, pp. 67–80

Gordillo, Gastón R., *Rubble: The Afterlife of Destruction* (Durham, NC: Duke University Press, 2014) <https://doi.org/10.1515/9780822376903>

Graeber, David, 'Radical Alterity Is Just Another Way of Saying "Reality": A Reply to Eduardo Viveiros de Castro', *HAU: Journal of Ethnographic Theory*, 5.2 (2015), pp. 1–41 <https://doi.org/10.14318/hau5.2.003>

Gray, John, 'Open Spaces and Dwelling Places: Being at Home on Hill Farms in the Scottish Borders', *American Ethnologist*, 26.2 (May 1999), pp. 440–60 <https://doi.org/10.1525/ae.1999.26.2.440>

Grossman, Zoltan, 'War and New US Military Bases', *CounterPunch*, 2 February 2002 <https://www.counterpunch.org/2002/02/02/war-and-new-us-military-bases/>

Haraway, Donna J., *Staying with the Trouble: Making Kin in the Chthulucene*, Experimental Futures: Technological Lives, Scientific Arts, Anthropological Voices (Durham, NC: Duke University Press, 2016) <https://doi.org/10.1215/9780822373780>

—— 'Symbiogenesis, Sympoiesis, and Art Science Activisms for Staying with the Trouble', in *Arts of Living on a Damaged Planet: Ghosts and Monsters of the Anthropocene*, ed. by Anna Lowenhaupt Tsing, Nils Bubandt, Elaine Gan, and Heather Anne Swanson (Minneapolis: University of Minnesota Press, 2017), pp. M25–M50

—— *When Species Meet by Donna Jeanne Haraway* (Minneapolis: University of Minnesota Press, 2008)

Hartman, Saidiya V., 'Venus in Two Acts', *Small Axe: A Caribbean Journal of Criticism*, 12.2 (2008), pp. 1–14 <https://doi.org/10.1215/-12-2-1>

Hartman, Saidiya V., and Frank B. Wilderson III, 'The Position of the Unthought', *Qui Parle*, 13.2 (2003), pp. 183–201 <https://doi.org/10.1215/quiparle.13.2.183>

Henig, David, 'Iron in the Soil: Living with Military Waste in Bosnia-Herzegovina', *Anthropology Today*, 28.1 (February

2012), pp. 21–23 <https://doi.org/10.1111/j.1467-8322.
2012.00851.x>

Hovannisian, Richard G., ed., *Armenian Tigranakert/Diarbekir and Edessa/Urfa* (Costa Mesa, CA: Mazda Publishers, 2006)

Human Rights Watch, 'Flooding South Lebanon: Israel's Use of Cluster Munitions in Lebanon in July and August 2006', 16 February 2008 <https://www.hrw.org/report/2008/02/16/flooding-south-lebanon/israels-use-cluster-munitions-lebanon-july-and-august-2006>

Hustak, Carla, and Natasha Myers, 'Involutionary Momentum: Affective Ecologies and the Sciences of Plant/Insect Encounters', *Differences*, 23.3 (2012), pp. 74–118 <https://doi.org/10.1215/10407391-1892907>

Ingold, Tim, 'The Temporality of the Landscape', *World Archaeology*, 25.2 (October 1993), pp. 152–74 <https://doi.org/10.1080/00438243.1993.9980235>

Ingold, Tim, and Jo Lee Vergunst, 'Introduction', in *Ways of Walking: Ethnography and Practice on Foot*, ed. by Tim Ingold and Jo Lee Vergunst (London: Routledge, 2008), pp. 1–20 (p. 12).

Jobson, Ryan Cecil, 'The Case for Letting Anthropology Burn: Sociocultural Anthropology in 2019', *American Anthropologist*, 122.2 (2020), pp. 259–71 <https://doi.org/10.1111/aman.13398>

Johannes Gutenberg-Universität Mainz, 'The Mainz Sand Dunes Landscape', last modified 5 January 2012 <https://www.botgarden.uni-mainz.de/outdoor-grounds/the-mainz-sand-dunes-landscape/>

Jones, Brennon, 'Southern Lebanon's Deadly Crop', *New York Times*, 12 October 2006

Jongerden, Joost, 'Elite Encounters of a Violent Kind: Milli İbrahim Paşa, Ziya Gökalp and Political Struggle in Diyarbekir at the Turn of the 20th Century', in *Social Relations in Ottoman Diyarbekir, 1870–1915*, ed. by Joost Jongerden and Jelle Verheij (Leiden: Brill, 2012), pp. 55–84 <https://doi.org/10.1163/9789004232273_004>

—— *The Settlement Issue in Turkey and the Kurds: An Analysis of Spatical Policies, Modernity and War* (Leiden: Brill, 2007) <https://doi.org/10.1163/ej.9789004155572.i-355>

Jongerden, Joost, and Jelle Verheij, eds, *Social Relations in Ottoman Diyarbekir, 1870–1915* (Leiden: Brill, 2012) <https://doi.org/10.1163/9789004232273>

Jung, Keun-Sik, 'The Construction of the Cold War Landscape and Tourism: The Possibilities and Limitations of its Peaceful Use', *Journal of Asian Sociology*, 48.3 (September 2019), pp. 287–319

Kaiser, Hilmar, 'Armenian Property, Ottoman Law and Nationality Policies', in *The First World War as Remembered in the Countries of the Eastern Mediterranean*, ed. by Olaf Farschid, Manfred Kropp, and Stephan Dähne, Beiruter Texte und Studien, 99 (Würzburg: Ergon-Verlag, 2006), pp. 49–71 <https://nbn-resolving.org/urn:nbn:de:gbv:3:5-91478>

Karaca, Banu, *The National Frame: Art and State Violence in Turkey and Germany* (New York: Fordham University Press, 2021) <https://doi.org/10.5422/fordham/9780823290208.001.0001>

Keller, Tait, 'The Mountains Roar: The Alps during the Great War', *Environmental History*, 14.2 (2009), pp. 253–74

Kévorkian, Raymond, *Le Génocide des Arméniens* (Paris: Odile Jacob, 2006)

Kévorkian, Raymond, and Paul Paboudjian, *Ermeniler: 1915 Öncesinde Osmanlı İmparatorluğu'nda*, trans. by Mayda Saris (Istanbul: Aras Yayıncılık, 2012)

Khayyat, Munira, *A Landscape of War: Ecologies of Resistance and Survival in South Lebanon* (Oakland: University of California Press, 2022) <https://doi.org/10.1525/9780520390003>

Khayyat, Munira, and Rabih Shibli, 'Tobacco Olives and Bombs: Reconfiguration and Recovery of Landscape in Postwar Southern Lebanon', in *The Right to Landscape: Contesting Landscape and Human Rights*, ed. by Shelley Egoz, Jala Makhzoumi, and Gloria Pungetti (Farnham, UK: Ashgate, 2012), pp. 263–76

Kim, Eleana J., 'Toward an Anthropology of Landmines: Rogue Infrastructure and Military Waste in the Korean DMZ', *Cultural Anthropology*, 31.2 (2016), pp. 162–87 <https://doi.org/10.14506/ca31.2.02>

Kohn, Eduardo, *How Forests Think: Toward an Anthropology Beyond the Human* (Berkeley: University of California Press, 2013) <https://doi.org/10.1525/9780520956865>

Kouymjian, Dickran, 'Confiscation and Destruction: A Manifestation of the Genocidal Process', *Armenian Forum*, 1.3
(1998), pp. 1–12

Kuyumcuyan, A., in *Tigris-Dikris Almanac* (Aleppo: Digranakerd Compatriotic and Reconstruction Union, 1946), p.
97

Kwek, Dorothy H. B., and Robert Seyfert, 'Affect Matters: Strolling through Heterological Ecologies', *Public Culture*, 30.1
(2018), pp. 35–59 <https://doi.org/10.1215/08992363-
4189155>

Lyons, Kristina, 'Chemical Warfare in Colombia, Evidentiary
Ecologies and Senti-actuando Practices of Justice', *Social
Studies of Science*, 48.3 (June 2018), pp. 414–37 <https://
doi.org/10.1177/0306312718765375>

—— 'Decomposition as Life Politics: Soils, Selva, and Small
Farmers under the Gun of the US-Colombian War on
Drugs', *Cultural Anthropology*, 31.1 (2016), pp. 56–81
<https://doi.org/10.14506/ca31.1.04>

MacLeish, Kenneth, and Zoë H. Wool, 'US Military Burn
Pits and the Politics of Health', *Medical Anthropology
Quarterly* (1 August 2018) <https://medanthroquarterly.
org/critical-care/2018/08/us-military-burn-pits-and-
the-politics-of-health/>

—— 'US Military Burn Pits and the Politics of Health', *Medical Anthropology Quarterly Critical Care Blog*, 2018
<https://medanthroquarterly.org/critical-care/2018/
08/us-military-burn-pits-and-the-politics-of-health/>
[accessed 24 March 2022]

Magdoff, Fred, and Chris Williams, 'Capitalist Economies Create Waste, Not Social Value', *Truthout*, 17 August 2017
<https://truthout.org/articles/capitalist-economies-
create-waste-not-social-value/> [accessed 22 March
2022]

Masco, Joseph, 'Mutant Ecologies: Radioactive Life in Post–
Cold War New Mexico', *Cultural Anthropology*, 19.4
(2004), pp. 517–50 <https://doi.org/10.1525/can.2004.
19.4.517>

Maynard, Robyn, and Leanne Betasamosake Simpson, *Rehearsals for Living* (Chicago, IL: Haymarket, 2022)

McKittrick, Katherine, *Demonic Grounds: Black Women and the Cartographies of Struggle* (Minneapolis: University of Minnesota Press, 2006)

Melamed, Jodi, 'Diagnosing Racial Capitalism', *Boston Review*, 10 September 2018 <https://bostonreview.net/forum_response/andrew-douglas-diagnosing-racial-capitalism/> [accessed 22 March 2022]

Mıgırdiçyan, Tovmas, 'Letter', *Nor Dikanagerd*, 20.3 (1938), pp. 9–11

Mgunt, Dikran, *ԱՄԻՏԱՅԻ ԱՐՁԱԳԱՆԳՆԵՐ* [Echoes of Amida] (Weehawken, NJ, Dikran Spear, 1950; repr. Antelias, Lebanon: Cilicia Bookstore, 2019)

Miroğlu, Orhan, *Hevsel Bahçesinde Bir Dut Ağacı: Mehmet Uzun'un Sunuşuyla Canip Yıldırım'la Söyleşi* (Istanbul: Everest Yayınları, 2010)

Morrison, Heidi, 'Review of Nadera Shalhoub-Kervorkian, Incarcerated Childhood and the Politics of Unchilding', *Journal of Palestine Studies*, 49.3 (Spring 2020), pp. 82–84 <https://www.palestine-studies.org/en/node/1650365> [accessed 22 March 2022] <https://doi.org/10.1525/jps.2020.49.3.82>

Muñoz, José Esteban, *The Sense of Brown*, ed. by Joshua Chambers-Letson and Tavia Nyong'o (Durham, NC: Duke University Press, 2020) <https://doi.org/10.1215/9781478012566>

Myers, Natasha, 'Becoming Sensor in Sentient Worlds: A More-than-Natural History of a Black Oak Savannah', in *Between Matter and Method*, ed. by Gretchen Bakke and Marina Peterson (London: Routledge, 2017), pp. 73–96 <https://doi.org/10.4324/9781003084792-5>

Naroyan, Mesrop, 'Open Letter', *Nor Dikaranagerd*, 21.2 (1938), pp. 9–10

Nash, Thomas, *Foreseeable Harm: The Use and Impact of Cluster Munitions in Lebanon; 2006* (London: Landmine Action, 2006)

Navaro, Yael, 'Affective Spaces, Melancholic Objects: Ruination and the Production of Anthropological Knowledge', *Journal of the Royal Anthropological Institute*, 15. 1 (March 2009), pp. 1–18 <https://doi.org/10.1111/j.1467-9655.2008.01527.x>

—— 'The Aftermath of Mass Violence: A Negative Methodology', *Annual Review of Anthropology*, 49.1 (2020), pp. 161–73 <https://doi.org/10.1146/annurev-anthro-010220-075549>

Nichanian, Marc, *The Historiographic Perversion*, trans. by Gil Anidjar (New York: Columbia University Press, 2009) <https://doi.org/10.7312/nich14908>

—— *Writers of Disaster: Armenian Literature in the Twentieth Century* (Princeton, NJ: Taderon Press, 2002)

Nixon, Rob, *Slow Violence and the Environmentalism of the Poor* (Cambridge, MA: Harvard University Press, 2013)

Öktem, Kerem, 'Incorporating the Time and Space of the Ethnic 'Other': Nationalism and Space in Southeast Turkey in the Nineteenth and Twentieth Centuries', *Nations and Nationalism*, 10.4 (2004), pp. 559–78 <https://doi.org/10.1111/j.1354-5078.2004.00182.x>

Öğüt, Tahir, and Çiğdem Çadırcı, 'Cumhuriyet Dönemine Geçiş Sürecinde Diyarbakır'da İktisadi-Mali ve Sosyal Yapı', *Gazi Akademik Bakış*, 7.13 (2013), pp. 141–70

Olwig, Kenneth, 'Performing on the Landscape versus Doing Landscape: Perambulatory Practice, Sight and the Sense of Belonging', in *Ways of Walking*, ed. by Ingold and Vergunst, pp. 81–92

Pearson, Chris, 'Researching Militarized Landscapes: A Literature Review on War and the Militarization of the Environment', *Landscape Research*, 37.1 (2012), pp. 115–33 <https://doi.org/10.1080/01426397.2011.570974>

Pörtner, Hans-Otto, Debra C. Roberts, and others, 'IPCC, 2022: Summary for Policymakers', in *Climate Change 2022: Impacts, Adaptation, and Vulnerability; Contribution of Working Group II to the Sixth Assessment Report of the Intergovernmental Panel on Climate Change*, ed. by Hans-Otto Pörtner, Debra C. Roberts, and others (Cambridge: Cambridge University Press, forthcoming) <https://www.ipcc.ch/report/ar6/wg2/downloads/report/IPCC_AR6_WGII_SummaryForPolicymakers.pdf> [accessed 22 March 2022]

Povinelli, Elizabeth, *Geontologies: A Requiem for Late Liberalism* (Durham, NC: Duke University Press, 2016) <https://doi.org/10.1215/9780822373810>

Puar, Jasbir K., *The Right to Maim: Debility, Capacity, Disability* (Durham, NC: Duke University Press, 2017) <https://doi.org/10.1215/9780822372530>

Rancière, Jacques, *Dissensus: On Politics and Aesthetics* (London: Bloomsbury Publishing, 2010)

—— 'Ten Theses on Politics', trans. by Davide Panagia and Rachel Bowlby, *Theory & Event*, 5.3 (2001) <https://doi.org/10.1353/tae.2001.0028>

Rappaport, Meron, 'IDF Commander: We Fired More Than a Million Cluster Bombs in Lebanon', *Haaretz*, 12 September 2006 <https://www.haaretz.com/1.4865651> [accessed 12 November 2022]

Rich, Gillian, 'The Best Defense Stocks for Today — and the Future', *Investor's Business Daily*, 14 March 2022 <https://www.investors.com/news/best-defense-stocks-to-buy/> [accessed 22 March 2022]

Rubaii, Kali, 'Birth Defects and the Toxic Legacy of War in Iraq', *Middle East Report*, 296 (Fall 2020) <https://merip.org/2020/10/birth-defects-and-the-toxic-legacy-of-war-in-iraq-296

Scott, James C., *Weapons of the Weak: Everyday Forms of Peasant Resistance* (New Haven, CT: Yale University Press, 2000)

Shalhoub-Kervorkian, Nadera, *Incarcerated Childhood and the Politics of Unchilding* (Cambridge: Cambridge University Press, 2019) <https://doi.org/10.1017/9781108555470>

Sharpe, Christina, *In the Wake: On Blackness and Being* (Durham, NC: Duke University Press, 2016) <https://doi.org/10.1215/9780822373452>

Shaw, Ian G. R., 'Scorched Atmospheres: The Violent Geographies of the Vietnam War and the Rise of Drone Warfare', *Annals of the American Association of Geographers*, 106.3 (2016), pp. 688–704 <https://doi.org/10.1080/00045608.2015.1115333>

Sheriff, Sarah, 'Unchilding of Palestinian Children', *Muslim News*, 28 June 2018 <https://muslimnews.co.uk/newspaper/human-rights/unchilding-palestinian-children/> [accessed 22 March 2022]

Simpson, Audra, *Mohawk Interruptus: Political Life Across the Borders of Settler States* (Durham, NC: Duke

University Press, 2014) <https://doi.org/10.1215/9780822376781>

Simpson, Leanne Betasamosake, *As We Have Always Done: Indigenous Freedom Through Radical Resistance* (Minneapolis: University of Minnesota Press, 2017) <https://doi.org/10.5749/j.ctt1pwt77c>

Sloterdijk, Peter, *Terror from the Air*, trans. by Amy Patton and Steve Corcoran, Semiotext(e) Foreign Agents Series (Los Angeles: Semiotext(e); distributed by MIT Press, 2009)

Springer, Simon, *The Anarchist Roots of Geography: Toward Spatial Emancipation* (Minneapolis: University of Minnesota Press, 2016) <https://doi.org/10.5749/minnesota/9780816697724.001.0001>

Stamatopoulou-Robbins, Sophia, *Waste Siege: The Life of Infrastructure in Palestine* (Stanford, CA: Stanford University Press, 2019) <https://doi.org/10.1515/9781503610903>

Starn, Orin, 'HERE COME THE ANTHROS (AGAIN): The Strange Marriage of Anthropology and Native America', *Cultural Anthropology*, 26.2 (2011), pp. 179–204 <https://doi.org/10.1111/j.1548-1360.2011.01094.x>

Stoetzer, Bettina, 'Ruderal Ecologies: Rethinking Nature, Migration, and the Urban Landscape in Berlin', *Cultural Anthropology*, 33.2 (2018), pp. 295–323 <https://doi.org/10.14506/ca33.2.09>

Strömsten, Henrik, 'Military and Nature: An Environmental History of Swedish Military Landscapes' (MA thesis, Uppsala University, 2016)

Suciyan, Talin, *The Armenians in Modern Turkey: Post-Genocide Society, Politics and History* (London: I.B. Tauris, 2016) <https://doi.org/10.5040/9780755609024>

Tachjian, Vahé, *Daily Life in the Abyss: Genocide Diaries, 1915–1918* (Oxford: Berghahn Books, 2017) <https://doi.org/10.2307/j.ctvw04f4m>

Taşğin, Ahmet, and Marcello Mollica, 'Disappearing Old Christian Professions in the Middle East: The Case of Diyarbakır Pushee-Makers', *Middle Eastern Studies*, 51.6 (2015), pp. 922–31 <https://doi.org/10.1080/00263206.2015.1044525>

Tîgrîs, Amed, and Yıldız Çakar, *Amed: Coğrafya, Tarih, Kültür* (Diyarbakır: Diyarbakır Büyükşehir Belediyesi Yayınları, 2015)

'Theater of Operations: The Gulf Wars 1991–2011', *The Museum of Modern Art*, 2019 <https://www.moma.org/calendar/exhibitions/5084> [accessed 1 April 2022]

Todd, Zoe, 'An Indigenous Feminist's Take On The Ontological Turn: "Ontology" Is Just Another Word For Colonialism', *Journal of Historical Sociology*, 29.1 (2016), pp. 4–22 <https://doi.org/10.1111/johs.12124>

Trouillot, Michel-Rolph, *Silencing the Past: Power and the Production of History* (Boston, MA: Beacon Press, 1995)

Tsing, Anna Lowenhaupt, *The Mushroom at the End of the World: On the Possibility of Life in Capitalist Ruins* (Princeton, NJ: Princeton University Press, 2015) <https://doi.org/10.1515/9781400873548>

Tsing, Anna Lowenhaupt, Andrew S. Mathews, and Nils Bubandt, 'Patchy Anthropocene: Landscape Structure, Multispecies History, and the Retooling of Anthropology: An Introduction to Supplement 20', *Current Anthropology*, 60.S20 (2019), pp. S186–97 <https://doi.org/10.1086/703391>

Tsing, Anna Lowenhaupt, Jennifer Deger, Alder Keleman Saxena, and Feifei Zhou, eds, *Feral Atlas: The More-Than-Human Anthropocene* (Stanford University Press, 2021) <https://doi.org/10.21627/2020fa>

Tsing, Anna Lowenhaupt, Nils Bubandt, Elaine Gan, and Heather Anne Swanson, eds, *Arts of Living on a Damaged Planet: Ghosts and Monsters of the Anthropocene* (Minneapolis: University of Minnesota Press, 2017)

Tuck, Eve, and K. Wayne Yang, 'Decolonization Is Not a Metaphor', *Decolonization: Indigeneity, Education & Society*, 1.1 (2012) <https://jps.library.utoronto.ca/index.php/des/article/view/18630> [accessed 9 March 2022]

Üngör, Uğur Ümit, *The Making of Modern Turkey: Nation and State in Eastern Anatolia, 1913–1950* (Oxford: Oxford University Press, 2011)

Üngör, Uğur Ümit, and Mehmet Polatel, *Confiscation and Destruction: The Young Turk Seizure of Armenian Property* (London: Bloomsbury Academic, 2011)

Vansintjan, Aaron, 'Going beyond the "Ecological Turn" in the Humanities', *Entitle Blog — A Collaborative Writing Project on Political Ecology*, 2016 <https://entitleblog.org/2016/03/01/going-beyond-the-ecological-turn-in-the-humanities/> [accessed 26 July 2019]

Vartanyan Dilaver, Aylin, 'From Longing to Belong to Shaping the Longing: Dwelling with Armenian Women in Istanbul' (PhD diss., European Graduate School, forthcoming)

Vega, Facundo, 'On Bad Weather: Heidegger, Arendt, and Political Beginnings', in *Weathering: Ecologies of Exposure*, ed. by Christoph F. E. Holzhey and Arnd Wedemeyer, Cultural Inquiry, 17 (Berlin: ICI Berlin Press, 2020), pp. 227–43 <https://doi.org/10.37050/ci-17_11>

Vergès, Françoise, 'Racial Capitalocene: Is the Anthropocene Racial?', in *Futures of Black Radicalism*, ed. by Gaye Theresa Johnson and Alex Lubin (London: Verso Books, 2017), pp. 72–82

——'Wandering Souls and Returning Ghosts: Writing the History of the Dispossessed', *Yale French Studies*, 118/119, 2010, pp. 136–54

Verheij, Jelle, 'Diyarbekir and the Armenian Crisis of 1895', in *Social Relations in Ottoman Diyarbekir*, ed. by Jongerden and Verheij (2012), pp. 85–147

Voyles, Traci Brynne, *Wastelanding: Legacies of Uranium Mining in Navajo Country* (Minneapolis: University of Minnesota Press, 2015) <https://doi.org/10.5749/minnesota/9780816692644.001.0001>

Weisel, Karl, 'Project Serves Soldiers and the Environment', US Army website, 23 February 2009 <https://www.army.mil/article/17299/project_serves_soldiers_and_the_environment>

Weston, Kath, *Animate Planet: Making Visceral Sense of Living in a High-Tech Ecologically Damaged World* (Durham, NC: Duke University Press, 2017) <https://doi.org/10.2307/j.ctv11cw43n>

Whiteman, Lou, 'Investing in Defense Stocks', *The Motley Fool*, 22 March 2022 <https://www.fool.com/investing/stock-market/market-sectors/industrials/defense-stocks/> [accessed 22 March 2022]

Wikipedia, s.v. 'Grosser Sand' (in German), last modified 18 September 2020 <https://de.wikipedia.org/wiki/Gro%C3% 9Fer_Sand>

—— 'Ultramarine', last modified 19 April 2021 <https://en. wikipedia.org/wiki/Ultramarine>

Woodward, Rachel, 'How Military Landscapes Work', in *Military Landscapes*, ed. by Ingrid Book and Carina Heden (Bergen: Bergen Kunsthalle, 2008), pp. 78–101

—— 'Military Landscapes: Agendas and Approaches for Future Research', *Progress in Human Geography*, 38.1 (February 2014), pp. 40–61 <https://doi.org/10.1177/ 0309132513493219>

Wynter, Sylvia, 'Unsettling the Coloniality of Being/Power/ Truth/Freedom: Towards the Human After Man, Its Overrepresentation — An Argument', *CR: The New Centennial Review*, 3.3 (Fall 2003), pp. 257–337 <https://doi.org/10. 1353/ncr.2004.0015>

Yadırgı, Veli, *The Political Economy of the Kurds of Turkey: From the Ottoman Empire to the Turkish Republic* (Cambridge: Cambridge University Press, 2017) <https://doi.org/10. 1017/9781316848579>

Yıldırım, Umut, 'Resistant Breathing: Ruined and Decolonial Ecologies in a Middle Eastern Heritage Site', *Current Anthropology*, forthcoming

—— 'Space, Loss and Resistance: A Haunted Pool-Map in South-Eastern Turkey', *Anthropological Theory*, 2019 <https://doi.org/10.1177/1463499618783130>

—— 'Spaced-Out States: Decolonizing Trauma in a War-Torn Middle Eastern City', *Current Anthropology*, 62.6 (2021), pp. 717–40 <https://doi.org/10.1086/718206>

Zavzavatcıyan B. Tovmas, 'Letter', *Nor Dikaranagerd*, 21 (1939), p. 5

Zentelis, Rick, and David Lindenmayer, 'Bombing for Biodiversity — Enhancing Conservation Values of Military Training Areas', *Conservation Letters*, 8.4 (July/August 2015), pp. 299–305 <https://doi.org/10.1111/conl.12155>

Notes on the Contributors

Jumana Emil Abboud is a Palestinian artist living and working in Jerusalem and London. She conjoins folklore with land-water mythologies and entanglements in the present, and works across drawing, workshopping, and wording to support imaginaries of the oppressed. Her creative motives emphasize a time and place where humans and more-than-humans are companions within storytelling and spirited waters. Her recent work has been presented in numerous exhibitions including at the 8th Thessaloniki Biennale (2023), 23rd Biennale of Sydney (2022), documenta 15 (2022), Seoul Museum of Art, South Korea (2019), Darat al Funun, Amman, Jordan (2017), Bildmuseet, Umeå, Sweden (2017), Baltic Centre for Contemporary Art, Newcastle, UK (2016), Khalil Sakakini Cultural Center, Ramallah (2016), and the 56th Venice Biennale (2015).

Marwa Arsanios has a practice that tackles structural and infrastructural questions using different devices, forms, and strategies from architectural spaces and their transformation and adaptability throughout conflict to artist run spaces and temporary conventions between feminist communes and cooperatives. Arsanios was a researcher in the Fine Art Department at the Jan Van Eyck Academie, Maastricht from 2010 to 2012. She is currently a PhD candidate at the Akademie der bildenden Künste in Vienna. Her most recent solo shows include Heidelberger Kunstverein, Germany (2023), Mosaic Rooms, London (2022), and Contemporary Arts Center, Cincinnati (2021). Her work has also been featured in numerous group exhibitions including: documenta 15 (2022), Mardin Biennial, Turkey (2022), the film programme at the 23rd Biennale of Sydney (2022), 3rd Autostrada Biennale, Pristina (2021), and 11th Berlin Biennale (2020). Her films have been screened at Cinéma du Réel, Paris (2021); Rotterdam Film Festival (2021); Film Fest, Hamburg (2020); FID Marseille (2015, 2019, and 2022).

Nadine Hattom was born in Baghdad, Iraq in 1980, and grew up in Abu Dhabi before migrating to Australia. She is an artist working with photography, sculpture, and installation. Taking a reading of landscape as a cultural process as her starting point, Hattom's work is an exploration of space and place, unravelling narratives of migration, region, representation, and landscape. Hattom studied Photomedia at the College of Fine Arts, Sydney. Her recent exhibitions include the Iraq Pavilion at the 57th Venice Biennale (2017), Arti et Amicitiae, Amsterdam (2017), Fotomuseum, Antwerp (2017), and the Marrakech Biennale 6 (2016). Hattom was selected for the 2018 BPA — Berlin program for artists. She currently resides and works in Berlin.

Munira Khayyat is associate professor of Anthropology at NYUAD in the United Arab Emirates. She was previously assistant professor of anthropology at the American University in Cairo and was a member of the Institute for Advanced Study in Princeton from 2018 to 2019. Her research revolves around ecologies of life in war and genealogies of empire. She is the author of *A Landscape of War: Ecologies of Resistance and Survival* (University of California Press 2022) and her essays have appeared in *American Ethnologist, Public Culture, JMEWS, Anthropology News,* and *HAU.*

Kali Rubaii is an assistant professor of anthropology at Purdue University. Her research explores the environmental impacts of militarism, namely how families in Anbar, Iraq struggle to survive and recover from transnational counterinsurgency projects. Her research focuses on the environmental impacts of less-than-lethal militarism, and how military projects (re)arrange political ecologies in the name of 'letting live'. She also traces toxic material relations that are reflective of warfare as a durable structure.

Françoise Vergès grew up on Réunion Island in an anticolonial feminist family, learning early on in life about coloniality and gender, race, and class as systemic systems of domination. She worked as a journalist and editor, and was an antiracist and feminist activist before getting her PhD in Political Theory at Berkeley University in 1995. She has written films about Maryse Condé and Aimé Césaire, organized decolonial visits in museums, co-founded the collective Decolonize the Arts (2015–2020), and was president of the French Committee for the Remembrance and History of Slavery (2008–2012), during which she fought for better recognition of the importance of slavery in the making of European modernity. Vergès writes about the afterlives of slavery and colonialism, the economy of extraction, the post-museum, feminisms, organizes workshops with artists and activists, and contributes to antiracist collectives. Her recent publications include *Programme de désordre absolu. Decoloniser le musée* (2023 [forthcoming in English 2024]), *De la violence coloniale dans l'espace public* (2021), *A Feminist Theory of Violence* (2021), and *A Decolonial Feminism* (2020).

Umut Yıldırım is an assistant professor of anthropology at the Geneva Graduate Institute, Switzerland. Her work explores transnational development programmes, expert networks, and aid policies in the Armenian/Kurdish region of Turkey, with a focus on the environmental effects of forced military migration and the political and ecological mobilization war generates. Her research is available in platforms such as Jadaliyya (2022), Current Anthropology (2021, 2023 fc), and Anthropological Theory (2019). She is currently working on her first monograph, titled *Low Intensities: Politics of War and Extraction in A Middle Eastern Capital.*

Index

Cultural Inquiry

EDITED BY CHRISTOPH F. E. HOLZHEY
AND MANUELE GRAGNOLATI